SWEET POTATO
SOUL

SWEET POTATO
SOUL

100 EASY VEGAN RECIPES FOR THE SOUTHERN FLAVORS OF SMOKE, SUGAR, SPICE, AND SOUL

JENNÉ CLAIBORNE

HARMONY BOOKS

Copyright © 2018 by Jenné Claiborne
Cover and interior photographs copyright © 2018 by
Sidney Bensimon

Published in the United States by Harmony Books, an
imprint of the Crown Publishing Group, a division of
Penguin Random House LLC, New York.
crownpublishing.com

Harmony Books is a registered trademark, and the Circle
colophon is a trademark of Penguin Random House LLC.

Library of Congress Cataloging-in-Publication Data has
been applied for.

ISBN 978-0-451-49889-2
Ebook ISBN 978-0-451-49890-8

Printed in China

Book and cover design by Sonia Persad

13

First Edition

for Nana

CONTENTS

INTRODUCTION

· ·

"Vegan food is soul food in its truest form. Soul food means to feed the soul. And, to me, your soul is your intent. If your intent is pure, you are pure." —Erykah Badu

I'VE GROWN ACCUSTOMED TO BEING asked if it's difficult to be a vegan from the South. Actually, I've come to enjoy the question. The curious questioners expect me to tell them how I nearly starve every time I visit my family in Georgia or how I'm embarrassed by the supposed Southern addiction to fried animal products and butter.

Instead, I tell them how much I adore eating Southern food and how practical it is to make our staples totally vegan. I tell them how each year at Christmas I indulge in vegan sweet potato pie, smoky collard greens, and stuffing with vegan sausage crumbles prepared by my nonvegan family. And how some of my favorite comfort foods are macaroni and "cheese," rice pudding, and sweet potato cinnamon rolls. Then I remind them that we Southerners are all about making things from scratch and that we have more pride than anyone else in the country for our regional produce like sweet potatoes, peaches, collard greens, and watermelon. I tell them about the many chefs who are embracing and building fantastic meals around Southern plants, not meat. And of course, I tell them how my great-grandparents from the South—and my ancestors from West Africa—ate mostly plant-based diets because it was efficient, reliable, and nutritious. Then I usually offer them a little Southern hospitality and invite them to try a Southern recipe made vegan. Maybe my sweet and savory Peach-

Date BBQ Jackfruit Sliders (page 135) with Coconut Collard Salad (page 74) on the side, and Cream Cheese Pound Cake (page 174) for dessert. If they weren't already convinced, that'll do the trick.

The truth is, no matter your background, you can be vegan and still enjoy the delicious flavors of your culture.

The intention of *Sweet Potato Soul* was planted in my nana's kitchen in the early 1990s, but it took until 2010, after much watering, to sprout.

I began cooking on my own when I was in elementary school. When I was seven, my mom and I moved out of Nana's cozy home and into a house of our own in the Atlanta suburbs. Since my mom didn't like to cook, she bought me a massive cookbook, at my request, and I found the perfect kid-friendly recipe: Szechuan chicken. I don't remember making anything but that one recipe, but I do remember the joy and pride I felt every time I'd serve it to my hardworking single mom.

Actually, my love of food and comfort in the kitchen began long before that. Some of my earliest memories take place in Nana's kitchen. She'd let me sit on the counter and watch her make biscuits or help her peel potatoes for Sunday morning home fries. She has always been one of the most supportive figures in my life, and she was the one who invited me into the kitchen to dream up my own creations. I can clearly recall mixing flour, baking soda, and nearly every spice in the cupboard just to see what would happen once we put it to fire. I also loved using the mailbox as an oven to bake mud cakes and pies. Imagine, a mailbox full of mud, and I never got in trouble. My whole life,

the kitchen has represented safety, creativity, and love.

Despite my love of food, I was a very picky kid. I loved watching Nana chop onions without a cutting board—all she needed was two hands and a paring knife—but I'd dare not eat them. I remember watching my mom spread peanut butter and being repulsed by the sight and smell. I later learned that I am allergic to peanuts, but I can't fall back on that excuse to explain my many other childish whims: the crust on sandwich bread, nuts of every kind, sour foods, coconut, salads, and most vegetables all landed on my no-eat list in those days. (Lest you stop reading here, rest assured, my tastes have since evolved!)

I moved up north to go to college. After four years of playing around in various college apartment kitchens, expanding my palate to include many of the foods I disliked as a child, and discovering countless other ingredients and cuisines, my love of food reached an all-time high. Despite being far from Nana's kitchen, I always maintained my love of Southern food and compared the quality of everything I made or ate at a restaurant to the amazing soul food I was raised on. Though my childhood diet was full of processed sugar and refined grains, my family also used fresh plant-based foods like collard greens, sweet potatoes, beans, and corn to make the most delicious meals. I was also raised a semivegetarian, meaning we ate birds and fish but avoided meat from mammals—red meat. We didn't buy into the myth that people need to eat meat for protein or other nutrients. Healthy food was plant-based. It's really no surprise I grew up and became a vegan chef.

In 2010, I graduated from Boston University's theater arts program and moved to New York City to become a working actress. In between auditions, callbacks, go-sees, and odd jobs, I started my food blog. Food and cooking had become my passion, and I thought a blog would be the perfect way to share it with the world. I called it *Sweet Potato Soul*. *Sweet Potato* because these tubers are manna from heaven and have always been my favorite food, and also because they're Southern, sweet, and healthy—just like me! And *Soul* pays tribute to the food I grew up eating, soul food made with love. At first, creating recipes for the blog was just a hobby. My main aspiration was to become a famous actress who would eventually write her own cookbook and maybe have a cooking

nutritional yeast, vegan "cheese," and Bragg Liquid Aminos. My dad's vegan family members would always show up to gatherings with vegan food—I especially remember my aunt Lorna's huge sheet cakes. Still, most of my family ate plenty of animal products, and I thought of veganism as a religious and spiritual endeavor, and since I wasn't a part of that religion, I did not see it as something for me.

Working at Peacefood opened my eyes. For the first time I met vegans who had chosen this lifestyle for ethical reasons. I learned about heinous abuses in the dairy, egg, and fishing industries, and I knew at once that I could no longer participate in such a cruel and exploitative system. Once I became vegan, I started learning more about the animal agriculture complex

"Trust in what you love, continue to do it, and it will take you where you need to go." —Natalie Goldberg

show (I take "dream big" seriously). Becoming vegan changed everything.

I went vegan in 2011 while working at an amazing vegan restaurant in New York City, Peacefood Café. I had become a vegetarian for health reasons a couple years prior—though I toggled between that and pescatarian—and Peacefood was the place where I could work between acting auditions and not have to serve meat. It wasn't my first exposure to veganism. My dad was raised vegan in the Hebrew Israelite community and to this day cooks primarily vegan. Because of him I was familiar with early vegan staples such as tofu, turmeric,

in the United States and other nations. I was shocked to learn that millions of land animals are killed every hour for food and that the largest contributor to greenhouse gas emissions is animal agriculture. It made so much sense when I realized how inefficient it is to get nutrients from animal products—nutrients that those animals get from plants! I learned about factory-farm runoff destroying local waterways and about cattle grazing contributing to deforestation in the Amazon rain forest (it's the leading cause!). Advocates of animal agriculture talk a lot about how factory farms have allowed for more people to consume calorie-rich

animal flesh, but they don't acknowledge the cruelty, exploitation of animals and workers, inefficiency, and environmental degradation that come along with it. Those who pine for a transition from factory farms to grass-fed and free-range livestock don't acknowledge that this way of feeding people is even less efficient than factory farming. You can't feed the world with grass-fed meat, but you can feed the world with plants.

Besides being ethical, leaps-and-bounds better for the environment, and a more efficient way to consume nutrients, the vegan lifestyle is also the healthiest way to live. You've seen the reports: *Study says people who eat a vegan diet live longer. . . . Research indicates plants help lower risk of cancer. . . . World Health Organization categorizes processed meat as a group 1 carcinogen along with tobacco smoking.* There's a new study every week proving the superior health benefits of a vegan diet. It is even useful in reversing and reducing the risk of extremely common diseases, including cancer, heart disease, diabetes, and Alzheimer's.

When I became vegan, health was not a motivator. A few weeks later, however, it became one. I had been suffering from gastrointestinal issues and discomfort for as long as I can remember, but shortly after becoming vegan, they all went away. It was as though I had flipped a switch. Over the years I've learned more and more about the countless health benefits of living a vegan lifestyle. Plants are full of healing nutrients that work synergistically to keep disease at bay and the body in balance. Since I didn't even think of myself as being unwell—I thought these issues were just something I had to live with—I was amazed to

feel the healing power of a vegan diet in my own body.

You see, once I became vegan the floodgates were open. I loved food before, but going vegan gave me reason to love it for its healing properties, its ability to prevent billions of animals from dying each year, and its power to transform the world. The passion I had for food before going vegan morphed into something that I have come to live and breathe. A month after becoming vegan, I decided I no longer wanted to be an actress. I wanted to help other people discover the vegan lifestyle. All of a sudden, *Sweet Potato Soul* had a real mission—to make it easy for people to enjoy delicious, familiar dishes without having to sacrifice their health or morals. I made up my mind to use my passion for vegan food and skills in the kitchen to start a personal-chef company in New York City, and my business, The Nourishing Vegan, was born. I also started coaching women on their vegan journey, teaching cooking classes all around New York, and sharing recipes via my YouTube channel. Over the years I've spread my message of veganism to thousands of people, and in talking to folks, one theme repeats itself no matter where I am: going vegan can be hard because it may seem as though you'll have to give up the foods you love the most, especially foods that are culturally meaningful.

Within a year of becoming vegan, I could no longer see animal products as food, and because of that I lost all craving for them. Still, it made me sad to sit at the dinner table on Christmas and not be able to enjoy my family's soul food. I can't remember what I ate that first Christmas as a vegan, but I remember promising myself that I would veganize and perfect all my favorite Southern dishes, like sweet potato pie, biscuits, filling, collard greens, candied yams, and everything in between. I was determined to prove to my family and to myself that animal products are not necessary to make Southern food. I tell you, it was not easy, but it has been one of the most rewarding tasks of my life. In veganizing Southern food, I have learned the hidden stories behind our most venerable dishes, the true origins of our favorite produce, and how vegan-friendly soul food has always been.

SOUTHERN FOOD

When most folks think of Southern food, they think of butter, deep-frying, and sugar. Specific Southern dishes that stand out are probably barbecue, fried chicken, buttermilk biscuits, cornbread, gumbo, and greens made with ham hock. But what do you know, Southern food is so much more than that and most of it (including the fried chicken and barbecue) can be made vegan.

Southern cuisine encompasses a very large and diverse part of the United States. From Louisiana to the Carolinas, it reflects the mixing of thousands of years of food culture from many different groups of indigenous Americans, Africans, and Europeans. There are some very famous influences on this cuisine—namely, slavery, Southern agriculture, and Southern produce. Look deeper and you'll find food connections between slaves and free blacks who came from the Caribbean to Georgia's

Sea Islands and to Louisiana. Or you'll discover conflicting theories regarding the origin of a dish like gumbo—was it West African, Choctaw, or French? A mix of the three? Southern food is like that: it's a fusion of many cultures, people, and circumstances, and there isn't one right way to make anything. Even staple dishes like cornbread or collard greens are made in a wide variety of ways depending on who's in the kitchen and what part of the South they or their people are from. In this cookbook we'll explore those histories and so much more.

You may be wondering, what's the difference between soul food and Southern food? In its academic definition, soul food is an African American culinary tradition with roots in the southern United States, but that only describes 1 percent of what it really is. Soul food is history, triumph, passion, prayer, purpose, and love. Soul food is quite literally food that feeds one's soul. It is Southern American classics like mac and cheese, black-eyed peas, and collard greens made with the memory of our African and enslaved ancestors, with the awareness of our rich history. Soul food is gumbo from the bayou and crab cakes from the coast. It's also the hybrid dishes created with regional produce as blacks moved north and west during the Great Migration.

The term *soul food* is fairly new. It came into popularity in the 1960s when many African Americans were expressing a sense of black pride. The word *soul* reflected a celebration of black culture—think soul music. The term may be new, but the history of soul food started hundreds of years ago in West Africa, where so much of our favorite "Southern" produce originated: peanuts, okra, black-eyed peas. As the

people from West Africa were stolen across the Atlantic as slaves, they brought nothing but their culture along with them. Despite an alien environment and the unimaginable violence and inhumanity of slavery, they held on to their African culture and created new foodways by blending traditional African produce with foods and cooking techniques influenced by indigenous Americans and European colonists. Their resourcefulness was incredible.

A misconception that exists to this day is that soul food is unhealthy and low class and should be reserved for special occasions in the company of other black folks. Southern African American food has bent and swayed had very little fresh food to enjoy themselves, and many were relegated to finding creative ways to turn the unwanted parts of animals and plants into nourishment—chitterlings, or pig intestines, are a classic example of this. However, the foundation of soul food lies more in the nutrient-rich foods that blacks were able to cultivate themselves in slave gardens and later on their own land. Black food has historically been vegetarian and has relied most on dark leafy greens (collards, turnip greens, and mustard greens), beans (especially black-eyed peas), whole grains (corn and rice), and starchy vegetables (sweet potatoes, turnips, potatoes). In West Africa, our ancestors have eaten similar

"While all soul food is Southern food, not all Southern food is 'soul.'"—Bob Jeffries

with the times. During slavery, black slaves were the cooks in the homes of white masters. The food they'd prepare for the slaveholders utilized fresh ingredients from the plantation garden or farm and would often be re-creations of European dishes. A notable embodiment of this phenomenon was James Hemings, Thomas Jefferson's slave chef. While serving as the ambassador to France, Jefferson brought Hemings along with him to Paris to learn French culinary techniques. Back home, Hemings re-created French dishes, one of which—macaroni and cheese—has become a staple in Southern kitchens.

Though slaves were cooking fresh food for their masters, depending on the situation, some plant-based foods for ages. Because produce is less energy-intensive, less expensive, more reliable, and nutritious, African diets have historically been based on starchy root vegetables like yams, greens, and groundnuts or peanuts. In fact, in most cultures around the world, meat did not become an everyday indulgence until very recently.

As American food became industrialized, so did Southern and soul food. Meat, dairy, and sugar became cheaper because of government subsidies, and as blacks moved north and away from Southern farmland during the Great Migration, fresh produce became harder to come by. Soul food contains all these elements: resourcefulness in times of shortage;

farm-fresh traditional foods from Africa, the Americas, and Europe; and boxed and canned food items produced in factories.

Soul food is a lot like another great cultural legacy of blacks in the South—jazz music. When you consume it, it feeds your soul. It borrows ingredients from other cultures to create something that's one of a kind. One may taste the melodies and notes in jazz and hear the flavors in soul food. And that is my intention with this book: to teach you to make food that not only tastes good and gives you necessary nutrition but is also food you can "hear," that makes you tap your foot and makes you feel alive.

MY SOUL FOOD PHILOSOPHY

I believe that the food you eat most should taste great and make you feel great. You shouldn't have to worry about suffering from chronic illness because you've eaten too much of the wrong thing, and you shouldn't have to rely on pills to function. At the same time, you shouldn't have to sacrifice taste and joy in order to stave off disease. You should be able to have your cake and eat it too, just maybe not every day.

Your diet can significantly lower or raise your risk of dying from the top killers in the United States—heart disease and cancer—so why take the risk? I believe we risk our lives for food because it has become the norm in our society. We all have a loved one who is suffering from a chronic illness, and almost everyone is eating a Standard American Diet high in processed ingredients, saturated fat, refined sugar, and chemical "food-like substances." I've talked to a number of people who believe they cannot expect to prevent a certain disease

because it runs in their family. The truth is that in most cases your genes are not your destiny; your lifestyle choices are. It takes a special person to go against the grain and choose a different way of living than what everyone around them is doing. If you are that person, I applaud you.

One way to oppose the Standard American Diet is to show people that they can have their favorite familiar foods and not risk being ostracized from their group. We should all be able to spend time with our families and enjoy a traditional meal without increasing our collective risk of cancer. This cookbook aims to satisfy the need for a healthier alternative to meat-based Southern and soul food. The same techniques can be used for foods from all different cultures. Jackfruit can always be used to replace pulled pork or chicken, flax can almost always replace eggs, coconut milk can always replace cream, and on and on. After all, before the rise of the industrialized food system most cultures around the world were plant-based.

It is also important to note that not all the recipes in this book are what I would consider healthy. Compared to the Standard American Diet they're superhealthy, but nutrition science and common sense shows us that the healthiest foods are those that have gone through the least amount of processing and manipulation. Recipes that use refined ingredients like white flour, white sugar, and vegan butter and techniques like deep frying should be eaten in moderation, say twice per week. The healthiest recipes are those that use wholesome vegetables, whole grains, and legumes, a few of my favorites being the Coconut Collard Salad (page 74), Low Country

Grits (page 60), Southern Buddha Bowl (page 131), New Orleans–Style Red Beans & Rice (page 140), Jackfruit Jambalaya (page 137), No-Bake Stone Fruit Cobbler (page 171), and Sweet Potato–Tahini Cookies (page 180).

In addition to making whole foods the base of your diet, I believe strongly in the power of a completely vegan lifestyle. Eating animal products, *even in moderation*, raises your risk for cancer, heart disease, and diabetes. While organic meat and dairy products do lower your exposure to toxins that concentrate in animal fat, the hormones that are linked to cancer are still there. Diets don't work, but lifestyle change does. If your goal is weight loss, you can find long-term success and overall health by adopting a healthy vegan diet that features the

familiar foods you love (just veganized), plus wholesome and delicious foods you've yet to discover. When you eat a whole food vegan diet you don't have to count calories or macronutrients because the food you consume has got it all: protein, fiber, vitamins, and minerals. Even better, you can eat more without feeling guilty because it's healthy; your body will signal when it has had enough—not the case with highly processed foods that lack nutrients.

Luckily we can create incredibly delicious food without dairy, eggs, and meat. If you're new to plant-based and vegan eating, get ready to discover a whole wide world of easy-to-find and affordable ingredients that help make your favorite foods special without having to use animal products.

FIVE HEALTHY FOOD RULES I LIVE BY

1. **Avoid all animal products.** The nutrients available in animals' flesh and excretions come from the plants that the animals eat. Why risk exposure to toxins and natural animal hormones when you can get all the protein, healthy fats, and micronutrients you need from plants? Plants can be used to replicate foods that traditionally use animals, like my Spicy Fried Cauliflower "Chicken" (page 152) or Happy Hearts "Crab" Cakes (page 129). Even more reason to leave animals off the menu.

2. **Eat your colors.** In the plant world, color is an indication of a plant's phytonutrients—plant nutrients that behave as antioxidants in your body. Highly processed foods lack these natural plant colors (manufacturers typically infuse them with artificial dyes instead) because they have been stripped away in the refining process along with other nutrients like minerals, fiber, and vitamins. As often as you can, choose colorful vegetables, beans, and whole grains like red kidney beans, black-eyed peas, brown rice, blue corn, purple cauliflower, orange sweet potatoes, and dark leafy greens.

3. **Don't count calories or protein.** When you eat a whole food vegan diet there is no reason to track nutritional numbers unless you are training for a bodybuilding competition. Eat a balance of whole grains, legumes, greens, vegetables, fruits, nuts, seeds, and healthy fats every day and you will reach your caloric and protein needs with ease. If you are pregnant or an athlete, you will need to eat more food to meet greater nutritional needs. Eat as much as you require to feel satiated, nourished, and energized. If you ever find yourself feeling weak or hungry, that is an indication to eat more wholesome food. Americans have an obsession with protein that is based in the strategic misinformation of clever animal product marketing—in fact, Americans eat a dangerous amount of animal protein, which has been linked to increased risk of cancer, heart disease, and diabetes. Protein deficiency is very rarely seen in developed countries, yet Americans and Europeans seem to fear it more than our top killers. All plant foods have protein, and as long as you are eating a wholesome diet, and enough food, you will get plenty of it.

4. **Go 80/20.** Eighty percent of the time I eat unprocessed whole foods; the other 20 percent of the time I indulge in meals and treats made with refined grains, sugar, and fat. It's a fulfilling and delicious way to eat. Because I make room for sweets, fried foods, and vegan junk food, I never feel deprived of those things. At the same time I never feel like I need to go on a diet or cleanse to reset.

5. **Make everything delicious.** Great tasting food does not require unhealthy processed ingredients, nor does it require a ton of time. Anyone who says so is simply unaware. You deserve delicious whether you are eating a salad, a simple snack, or Thanksgiving dinner. One of my favorite things about fresh fruit and vegetables is that they are full of flavor on their own without having to add tons of seasoning to them. Can't say the same for animal products. Take the time to learn how to make your daily meals delicious, and use this cookbook to help guide you along the way.

WHAT TO EXPECT FROM THIS BOOK

In the pages to follow, get ready to learn about creative techniques to make old favorites, the health benefits of your favorite Southern produce, and the origin stories of some of the South's most iconic foods. First, you'll find information about what tools you need to get started and guidelines for shopping for vegan staples and stocking your pantry. Then I describe the nutrient values and unique health benefits of the core soul food ingredients that you'll be using throughout this book. And finally, the main event: one hundred delicious recipes covering breakfast, salads, soups, mains, greens and other sides, baked treats, desserts, and drinks, perfected over my years in the kitchen, meant to be made and eaten with love.

Enjoy!

TOOLS TO STOCK YOUR SOUL KITCHEN

In this section, I'll help you get ready to make these amazing recipes by stocking your kitchen with the essentials. Before we move on to the recipes, let's go over the kitchen tools and pantry staples I recommend for ultimate soul kitchen success. It isn't necessary to acquire all these tools right away, but they do come in handy and make cooking more efficient and enjoyable. Don't worry about stocking your pantry right away either. As you move through these recipes, you'll naturally acquire new spices, flours, beans, and grains. Even better, most of the pantry staples are familiar ingredients that you may have in your kitchen already. Let's start with the tools.

CHEF'S KNIFE

This is one of the most important kitchen tools. A sharp, high-quality chef's knife will allow you more efficiency, precision, and safety when cutting vegetables. I recommend a sturdy 8-inch chef's knife. Be sure to keep it sharpened: invest in a knife sharpener or take it to a professional.

PARING KNIFE

Old-school cooks can use a paring knife like a boss. My nana uses one to hand-dice onions, potatoes, celery, and just about everything else—no cutting board required. However, I leave the handheld-chopping technique to the OGs. For our purposes I recommend this small, thin knife for stemming greens and mushrooms and other precision cutting. If you feel comfortable using a chef's knife for exact cuts, then this knife may not be necessary.

CUTTING BOARD

Don't have a cutting board? Drop everything and order one right away. If you only cook vegan food, you don't have to worry about cross-contaminating cutting boards, so just one board should do. Otherwise, you may need more. Look for a large, sturdy cutting board that can be used on both sides—one side for fruits, and the other for vegetables. A good cutting board should last for years and will keep your knives from losing their sharpness unreasonably fast.

WOODEN SPOONS

Cooking wouldn't be as fun without a set of assorted wooden spoons. Every kitchen should have spoons for stirring, scraping, and scooping. I prefer to use wooden spoons over plastic or metal because they are heat-resistant and sturdy, won't scratch pans, last forever, and feel best in your hand.

FLEXIBLE EXTRAWIDE SPATULA

You'll need a good spatula to flip your vegan pancakes. I also use mine to effortlessly flip Sweet Potato Burgers (page 156) and scoop up roasted vegetables. Make sure yours is heat-resistant. I prefer the plastic ones for their flexibility.

DUTCH OVEN

A heavy-bottomed, enamel-coated pot is as invaluable as a cast-iron skillet. Use it for soups, stews, beans, greens, and even for baking bread and deep-frying. The one downside to this pot is its weight—you will get a mini-workout every time you plop it down on your stovetop or remove it from your oven. Like a cast-iron skillet, a good cast-iron enamel-coated dutch oven will last for generations with proper tender love and care.

CAST-IRON SKILLET

For the ultimate Southern cooking experience, use a well-seasoned cast-iron skillet for almost everything from frying pancakes to cooking greens. It's also great to use in the oven for baking and roasting. The beauty of a cast-iron skillet is in its effortless nonstick surface and the fact that it's the only pan you need. Plus, my nana always says that cooking with one fortifies your food with a safe and healthy serving of iron. I paid around $40 for my 12-inch skillet. A well-cared-for skillet can stay in your family for generations.

Caring for a cast-iron skillet may seem intimidating, but it need not be. Follow these tips for perfect cast-iron care:

1. Never clean your skillet with soap. *Never!* Use a bristled brush or chemical-free scouring pad to remove residue from the pan. Soap will cause the skillet to lose its season and to rust.

2. If the caked-on food won't come off with dry scrubbing, add about ½ inch of water to the skillet and bring to a simmer. Use a wooden spoon or wooden spatula to scrape the food as it loosens with the boiling water. Once all the food is loose, pour the water out, and allow the skillet to cool before cleaning it the normal way.

3. Never let your skillet soak. Prolonged exposure to water will cause the skillet to rust.

4. After cleaning the skillet, dry it with a clean kitchen towel and then place it on the stove over low heat to thoroughly dry for at least 5 minutes. Lastly, use a paper towel to coat the skillet with about a teaspoon of a neutral oil.

FOOD PROCESSOR

This machine is invaluable. With it you can chop, shred, mince, and so much more. You can use it to make creamy dips, chunky vegan Happy Hearts "Crab" Cakes (page 129), and delicious desserts. I recommend a medium to large food processor. As you begin to use it more often, you'll appreciate the extra capacity of a larger machine.

HIGH-SPEED BLENDER

A good blender should produce a creamy dish without having to blend for too long and risk overheating. Use it to make perfect smoothies, blended soups, dressings, sauces, and more. High-speed blenders are certainly more expensive than slower blenders, but they are often worth the investment and will last longer. There are many on the market, so be sure to compare machines before investing.

SHEET PANS

For roasting, toasting, and baking, it's crucial to have at least two rimmed sheet pans. The standard size is 15 × 21 inches, but get whatever fits into your oven. A good sheet pan should last for years, but use parchment paper or a silicone mat to protect it when baking and to prolong its life.

BAKING PAN

Baking pans come in a wide range of sizes and shapes, but a basic 9 × 9-inch or 8 × 8-inch pan with 2-inch walls will work for everything from brownies to mac and "cheese." I recommend having at least two baking pans.

WAFFLE IRON

I admit, this isn't a life-or-death kitchen appliance that you'll use daily—though you could. However, homemade waffles are an absolute treat, and you're going to love my Sorghum Cornmeal Waffles (page 53).

PARCHMENT PAPER AND/OR SILICONE MAT

To save cleanup time, I never bake or roast directly on a sheet pan but instead use either parchment paper or a silicone mat, which prevents food from sticking. Look for parchment paper at any grocery store. Silicone mats can be found online or at kitchen stores.

SOUTHERN PANTRY STAPLES

BEANS & OTHER LEGUMES

For thousands of years, beans have been the protein of choice for cultures all around the world. They're easy to grow and very nutritious. Beans are an excellent source of fiber, protein, iron, magnesium, folate, and antioxidants. They've been studied extensively for their role in lowering the risk of heart disease and cancer. They're also a great source of prebiotics, or resistant starch, that is metabolized by the healthy bacteria in our gut to support overall physical and mental health.

I recommend preparing your beans at home instead of relying on canned beans (see Perfect Pot o' Beans on page 125). Home-cooked beans are fresher and more nutritious and have a better flavor and texture. They're also less expensive and supereasy to make. Most dried beans should be soaked overnight before cooking, but black-eyed peas and lentils are an exception to that rule. If you have issues digesting beans, take that as a sign that you should be eating more of them. Beans contain sugars that are fermented in the colon and

either promote the growth of healthy bacteria or make their way out as gas. By gradually increasing your consumption of beans, your body will be able to use the fermented sugars to promote these healthy bacteria that keep cancer at bay, and you will no longer have discomfort after eating them.

BLACK-EYED PEAS The quintessential Southern legume is the black-eyed pea, but it has been a staple on dinner tables throughout the world for thousands of years. Originally cultivated in West Africa, it made its way to Egypt, the Middle East, Asia, and Europe before ending up in the Americas in the 1700s. The black-eyed pea is a great nitrogen-fixing crop, and when used in crop rotation, it contributes to healthy soil. The plant grows well in warm climates and has long been prized for being drought-resistant. If you only know black-eyed peas from New Year's Day stew, you're missing out on their wonderful versatility. These tasty two-toned beans are also very nutritious—like all beans they provide a great source of fiber, protein, magnesium, and iron.

BUTTER BEANS (aka Lima Beans)
The large and luscious butter beans we love down south were first cultivated in the Andes more than four thousand years ago, though other varieties have been cultivated for more than seven thousand years. Though they were a mainstay in the diets of pre-Columbian Americans, butter beans—along with potatoes, tomatoes, corn, and many other American crops—fast became a household name around the world after 1492. In the Americas, beans have historically been grown alongside maize—corn—and consumed with it to make a complete nutrient-rich meal. These beans are particularly well suited for cultivation in warm climates, like the southern United States, where they've become a staple food. Besides providing fiber, protein, iron, and magnesium, they're also a great source of copper, manganese, and folate.

KIDNEY BEANS (aka Red Beans)
Like limas, kidney beans originated in the Americas, where they have been a staple food for thousands of years. They share a common bean ancestor with black beans, pinto beans, navy beans, and most other beans we know today. In Southern cuisine, kidney beans are most often paired with rice, as in my New Orleans–Style Red Beans & Rice (page 140)—one of my favorite healthy comfort foods.

Kidney beans, like other beans, are an excellent source of soluble fiber. This type of fiber creates a bulking action in our intestines and helps remove toxins, lower bad cholesterol, keep us full, and balance blood sugar. Kidney beans are high in lignans, a type of phytoestrogen, which acts as a powerful antioxidant in our bodies. Lignans are also known for their anticarcinogenic and anti-inflammatory effects. Diets high in fiber are usually high in this compound.

Uncooked kidney beans are not safe to eat because they contain a toxin called phytohemagglutinin. They should be soaked overnight and cooked until tender (45 to 90 minutes) before consuming.

POLE BEANS (aka Green Beans)
These unripened and unshelled beans were first cultivated in Central America. Today most green beans are grown in China, but they still have a special place in American kitchens and

gardens. The green bean's most popular use in American cooking is probably green bean casserole, but my favorite way to eat them is freshly harvested and tossed with my dad's famous salad dressing (see Pop's Tangy Green Bean Salad on page 71). Since they're green and unripened, green beans have a different nutritional profile than dry beans. They're high in vitamins K and C and—surprisingly—beta-carotene. Like other whole foods, they're also high in a number of phytonutrients and antioxidants. Note that while fresh beans are great, frozen green beans also maintain a high amount of their original nutritional value.

LENTILS   Though they aren't a particularly Southern food, lentils play a huge role in vegan soul cooking. Their small size, hearty texture, and high protein content make them terrific replacements for meat in recipes. Lentils, which originated in central Asia, are one of the oldest cultivated crops that we're aware of. They're legumes, or pulses, just like beans, but their size, different origin, and unique nutritional profile put them into a category of their own. Little ol' lentils rival soybeans for the highest legume protein content, and they boast impressive amounts of zinc, potassium, and folate. Lentils need not be soaked before cooking.

PEANUTS   My favorite fact about peanuts is that George Washington Carver had recipes for mock chicken, mock duck, and a nondairy milk using this legume in the early 1900s. As many schoolchildren learn, Carver was the "father of the peanut." He was an African American botanist, inventor, environmentalist, and both professor and researcher at the Tuskegee Institute, but he's most famous for his role in using peanut plants to restore cropland that had been depleted by cotton and for inventing an incredible number of uses for peanuts.

Peanuts are inexpensive, available worldwide, and healthy—they're high in B vitamins, manganese, zinc, magnesium, and protein.

The peanuts we grow and most commonly eat in the United States originated in what is now northern Argentina. They're actually legumes, not nuts at all, despite the name. Groundnuts are a similar plant that originated in West Africa. (The term *groundnut* is also sometimes used to refer to peanuts.) Groundnuts have been used in West African cooking for thousands of years, and African slaves who were brought to the Americas brought along their custom of boiling them. Boiled peanuts are now one of the most typical Southern foods you can imagine. Unfortunately, I am allergic to peanuts (only those grown in the United States). There aren't many peanut-centric recipes in this book, but if you're a fan, feel free to use peanuts in place of nuts.

STAPLE GRAINS

Around the world whole grains have maintained their role as the foundation for a nourishing diet for thousands of years. When the staple grain in Europe was wheat, in the Americas it was corn and in Asia it was rice. Whole grains are a fantastic source of fiber, B vitamins, minerals, protein, antioxidants, and calories. Without this reliable source of nutrition, it can be argued that the greatest advancements in humankind would never have happened. Whole civilizations were built around the human potential they afforded. Whole grains were a world-changing discovery, and a couple very important ones make up the basis for the Southern diet.

CORN (aka Maize)   The history and global domination of corn deserves a book of its own, and I'm sure many have been written. The history of this ubiquitous crop takes us back more than eight thousand years to when it was domesticated in present-day Mexico. It's hard to believe, but corn descends from a tiny wild grass with a hard kernel. Through selective breeding, indigenous Americans created something far more similar to the corn we love today and spread it north and south throughout the Americas long before the first Europeans arrived.

For slaves, corn was perhaps the most common food ration because it was cheap, readily available, and easy to grow. Black people borrowed ways of preparing corn and cornmeal from Native Americans, and dishes like cornbread, corn pone, and grits became their mainstays.

These days corn isn't usually thought of as a health food, but it very well could be. This humble grain boasts a number of antioxidants, tons of fiber and protein, and B vitamins, which are crucial for energy.

TYPES OF CORN EATEN IN THE SOUTH

Cornmeal: Made from dried and ground corn kernels, cornmeal is most commonly used for cornbread. Varieties are white cornmeal, yellow cornmeal, stone-ground, and steel-ground.

Grits: Coarse-ground cornmeal used to make a creamy porridge. White or yellow grits can be purchased.

RICE   We think of rice as being specifically Asian, but a different species of the grain has been cultivated in West Africa for thousands of years. When slaves were brought to the Americas, so was African rice, and Europeans exploited the skills and abilities of their captives to create a thriving economy. In the United States, African rice especially grew well along the South Carolina coastal delta, in what is known today as the Low Country. As higher-yielding Asian rice spread in popularity, it replaced African rice throughout the Americas.

After the switch from African to Asian rice, the crop continued to be grown in the South and maintained its integral role in the region's cuisine. When cornbread isn't the main grain in a meal, rice will be. Throughout the South, stews like gumbo or red beans are served with rice, and rice is turned into sweet desserts and breakfasts like rice pudding. Rice-cooking styles have been influenced by African, Caribbean, French, and Spanish cuisine.

SOUTHERN FRUITS & VEGETABLES

Before the advent of agriculture around the world, humans relied on fresh fruits and vegetables for the bulk of our nutrient needs. A healthy diet is not complete without these foods because they provide us with important vitamins, minerals, phytonutrients, antioxidants, protein, and fiber. A diet high in fresh fruits and vegetables is associated with a lower risk of cancer, heart disease, autoimmune disease, obesity, and diabetes. Always keep your kitchen stocked with fresh and frozen fruits and vegetables. Fruits and veggies that are frozen at their peak of freshness maintain most of the nutrients they had at harvest time.

WATERMELON Modern watermelon has its roots in Africa, most likely North Africa, though varieties of wild melons similar to what we enjoy today grow throughout the continent. For millennia it has been enjoyed in Egypt, the Middle East, Asia, and Europe. Along with so many other crops, European colonists brought watermelon to the Americas, where it became a popular crop thanks to how easy it is to grow, its sweetness, and its refreshing quality.

Of course, watermelon is also connected with racist stereotypes, which took on their current significance around the time of emancipation. Southern whites felt threatened by the sight of proud newly freed people enjoying and selling watermelon and quickly began to create the caricatures of lazy childish blacks too focused on watermelon to do anything else in life—and thus not ready for or deserving of freedom.

Despite the disturbing tropes and racist baggage, watermelon is a Southern staple. During hot and humid summers, watermelon's high water content helps you stay hydrated and energized. Watermelon is high in the antioxidant lycopene, citrulline (an important amino acid), vitamin C, potassium, copper, and B vitamins.

Like all fruits and vegetables, watermelon is best when it is in season—in this case, that means from May to September. Choose a watermelon that is heavy for its size and has a large yellow spot on its "belly."

PEACHES I'm a Georgia girl, aka a Georgia Peach, so of course they're my favorite fruit. The best peaches in the South come from the Peach State, where they've been grown since the mid-1500s when they were introduced to the Georgia coast by Franciscan monks.

Despite their presence in the American South for so long, peaches did not achieve market appeal until the mid-1800s. During slavery, southern landowners were dependent on King Cotton, a labor-intensive crop. Without free labor, growers were forced to find alternative crops like peach trees to replace cotton.

In Southern kitchens, peaches are often served fresh, in a fruit cobbler, or as a preserve. Peaches are high in cancer-fighting polyphenols, lutein, vitamin C, vitamin A, antioxidants, and fiber. Choose peaches that are heavy for their size and have a vibrant color. They can ripen on your kitchen counter. Peaches are in season from May to September.

BLACKBERRIES Though they're grown throughout the United States and the world, blackberries have carved out a special place in Southern cuisine. Blackberries are used in cobblers, preserves, and syrups or just eaten fresh. Their dark color represents incredible cancer-fighting antioxidants called anthocyanins, which they have more of than most other fruits in the world. Blackberries are also a great source of vitamin C and fiber.

PLUMS Plums are in the same family as peaches, though in the South they're the less popular of the two. You'll find luscious varieties of plums at Southern farmers' markets that can be eaten fresh for a snack, added to cakes and muffins, preserved, or used for refreshing sorbet. Their dark purple pigmented skin packs a serious antioxidant punch, and plums are a great source of potassium and vitamin C. They're also a terrific source of fiber, so eat up!

SWEET POTATOES At the heart of Southern and soul food is the sweet potato: nutritious, delicious, beautiful, and abundant. By now you know that it is my favorite vegetable, but my love of this tuber is shared by people throughout the region and increasingly the whole United States.

Like all potatoes, sweet potatoes originated in the Americas and were introduced to Europeans and Africans thousands of years after their earliest cultivation, most likely in Peru. Across the ocean in West Africa, yams were a staple food. Though the two tubers are not related, slaves in the New World embraced sweet potatoes for their high starch content, ease to grow, and nutritional value and used them in a variety of preparations. At the base of sweet potato preparations was the simple baked potato wrapped in leaves and roasted with hot ashes (a style of cooking that was also used to make cornbread). Sweet potatoes made their way throughout the South and have long been treasured for their high yields.

Sweet potatoes are one of the most versatile foods on the planet. Traditionally, Southerners have used them baked and plain, in pies and casseroles. George Washington Carver was a huge proponent of expanding sweet potato cropland and invented unique and delectable ways to consume them: mock chicken with peanuts, sweet potato molasses, sweet potato vinegar, and so much more! (You can still find many of these historical treasures floating around the Internet, for example on the Tuskegee Institute's and the National Park Service's websites.) The sky's the limit when it comes to what you can make with sweet potatoes, as you'll soon find out in this cookbook—my favorite recipes include Sweet Potato Pancakes (page 52), Sweet Potato–Pecan Cinnamon Rolls (page 65), Sweet Potato–Parsnip Bisque (page 95), and Sweet Potato Burgers (page 156).

Types of Sweet Potatoes Most of us are aware of one or maybe two varieties of sweet potatoes: orange-fleshed and white-fleshed. But allow me to blow your mind: there are over a hundred different cultivars around the world. The differences range from bright purple to creamy white flesh, moist to super-starchy, and pink to gray skin. Since you probably won't find much variety at your local market, the recipes in this book call for the common sweet potato, the one with orange flesh and pinkish-brown skin.

WHAT'S THE DIFFERENCE BETWEEN SWEET POTATOES AND YAMS?

Sweet potatoes belong to the morning glory family and are usually orange and sweet with moist, starchy flesh. They are distantly related to potatoes, but they are not nightshades. Sweet potatoes and yams are not at all related. Yams are native to Africa and Asia and have starchy white flesh and gray-brown skin. They aren't nearly as nutritious as sweet potatoes and have a much lower yield. Sweet potato growers in the South started calling their potatoes yams as a marketing ploy to distinguish orange-fleshed from white-fleshed ones, and to this day we're still using *yams* to refer to certain types of sweet potatoes—Jewel yams and Garnet yams, most notably. It is said that the word *yam* was chosen because blacks in the South used this term for sweet potatoes, a holdover from African slaves.

VARIETIES
❧ *of* ❧
SWEET POTATOES
·All Can Be Found in the United States·

Beauregard   This is the most common commercial variety in the United States, but it's only been around since 1987 (my birth year). These taters are very easy to grow, high-yielding, and popular for their sweet and tender flesh. I use them in everything from Sweet Potato Skillet Home Fries (page 58) to Sweet Potato Yeast Donuts (page 177) to Sweet Potato Burgers (page 156).

Garnet   You'll see these, along with Jewels, referred to as yams, but they're sweet potatoes all the way. Garnet "yams" have a deep orange flesh and maroon-tinted skin, reflecting their very high levels of beta-carotene. They have a high water and sugar content, and their starchy flesh maintains a whole lot of creaminess and moistness when cooked. These are my favorite yams for baking whole or using in Nana's Sweet Potato Pie (page 165).

Jewel   With such a lovely name, you know these have got to be good. Jewel "yams" are long and elegant-looking, with smooth skin. When cooked the flesh is richly orange, sweet, and light. I especially like using Jewels for Sweet Potato Green Bean Casserole (page 148).

O'Henry   White-fleshed, creamy, and sweet, this cultivar is a close cousin of the Beauregard. Because of its white flesh, it is often used in place of white potatoes, which I think is a terrific idea. While O'Henrys are more nutrient-dense than white potatoes, their white flesh means they don't boast high levels of beta-carotene like other sweet potatoes.

Okinawan   These are perhaps the most unique sweet potatoes. The skin on Okinawans is nearly white, but inside the flesh is deep bright purple! I first tried these supersweet taters at my vegan restaurant job, and when I saw how bright purple they were, I couldn't believe they weren't artificially colored. Actually these beauties are all-natural, and their stunning flesh is an indication of high levels of anthocyanins—potent phytonutrients that are known to protect our bodies from disease. These sweet potatoes are rare, but look for them in Asian markets or purchase them online.

Porto Rico   These sweet potatoes have pinkish-colored skin and flesh, but otherwise are similar to Beauregards: moist, creamy, and sweet. Before understanding that they are a different variety, I thought they were uncured sweet potatoes. Curing sweet potatoes allows them to turn some of their starches into sugar and form calluses over cuts and nicks, which will prevent them from spoiling. When you buy sweet potatoes at the store, they have already been cured.

Japanese Satsumaimo   Called simply Japanese sweet potatoes in the United States, these have purplish skin and creamy white flesh. Compared to typical American sweet potatoes, these are sweeter and starchier. In Japan you can buy this type of sweet potato stone-roasted on the street and even at convenience stores like 7-Eleven. It is also used in a number of sweets and *mochi*.

Korean Goguma   In Korea the sweet potatoes are sweeter. Like in Japan, roasted sweet potatoes are a popular street food, especially in winter. Korean Goguma (*goguma* means "sweet potato") has a cream-colored flesh and brownish skin. Its delicious flavor is described as being similar to chestnuts. There are also purple Korean sweet potatoes, which have starchier, very sweet flesh.

Stokes Purple   This is a newer variety that became commercially available in 2012. Stokes Purple sweet potatoes have brilliant purple skin and flesh. Like Okinawan sweet potatoes, the purple indicates high levels of health-promoting anthocyanins. They have an earthy flavor and lower moisture content than orange-fleshed sweet potatoes.

Still, I think it's worth exploring some of the other varieties of the sweet potato. This humble tuber has been cultivated for millennia in the Americas and made its way around the entire world following European conquest. Throughout the centuries, sweet potatoes have been prized for their resistance to drought, ease of growing, and nutritional value. Today there may be dozens of cultivars of sweet potatoes, but they all have two things in common: they're delicious and versatile!

Sweet potatoes are a certified superfood! Their bright orange flesh tells you that they are a terrific source of beta-carotene (which the body converts to vitamin A), an important antioxidant for cardiovascular health, skin health, eye health, cell communication, immune support, and fighting inflammation. Sweet potatoes are also a terrific source of vitamin C, B vitamins, potassium (way better than bananas), copper, and manganese, and they are great for lowering inflammation, which can lead to chronic disease and cancer. Even more, these starchy gems are great for regulating our blood sugar levels thanks to their fiber and the ability to trigger the body to release adiponectin, a protein hormone that regulates insulin metabolism. Make sure to keep the skin on when you can for an extra boost of phytonutrients and fiber. Sweet potatoes even contain protein (about 4 grams per cup) and plenty of energy-boosting carbohydrates, making them an all-round perfect food.

How to pick, store, and prepare sweet potatoes   Select sweet potatoes that are firm, have uniform skin (whether smooth or slightly rough depending on the cultivar), seem heavy for their size, and are properly stored. Sweet potatoes should never be stored in the refrigerator. At the store they should be stored in a cool, dry area. At home they should be stored in a cool, dark area and never in plastic.

On the pages to come you'll see plenty of recipes calling for sweet potatoes. Let's set some guidelines for preparing your taters.

Sweet potato measurements   When a recipe calls for a medium sweet potato, I am referring to a tuber that is about the length of a woman's hand from palm to fingertip (about 5 inches) and about 4 fingers wide (about 2½ inches). Grocery stores tend to carry this size most often, so don't expect to have to sort through large bins to find what you're looking for.

When cooked whole, a medium sweet potato will yield about 1 cup of flesh. So 1 cup of sweet potato is about 1 medium sweet potato.

Baked and mashed sweet potatoes   I call for mashed sweet potato in many of the recipes in this book. This refers to the creamy flesh of the sweet potato, which can be mashed with a fork to remove lumps before using in a recipe. My favorite way to prepare mashed sweet potato is to bake the tuber whole. Poke a few fork holes in the potato, and then coat it with a very thin layer of a neutral oil. Line a sheet pan or baking pan with parchment paper and bake at 375°F for an hour. (Note that smaller sweet potatoes will bake more quickly.) The potatoes should be soft to the touch, and their caramelized sugars will seep out. Let the potato cool before scooping the flesh out of the skin, mashing until creamy, and using in a recipe. I recommend cooking a whole bunch of sweet potatoes at a time. The extra potatoes can be kept fresh in the fridge for a snack, meal addition, or for future baking. They'll keep for about 5 days. You can eat them cold or reheat them in the microwave or oven.

You can also quickly prepare mashed sweet potato in the microwave. Simply poke a few fork holes in the potato, wrap the potato in a sheet of dampened paper towel, and microwave on high for 7 to 10 minutes. Let the potato cool before scooping out the flesh, mashing, and using in a recipe.

Lastly, you can prepare mashed sweet potatoes by steaming. Place sweet potatoes in a steaming basket, tightly cover, and steam until tender all the way through, about 30 minutes. Let the potato cool before scooping out the flesh, mashing it thoroughly, and using it in a recipe. This method is my least favorite because the sugars do not caramelize during steaming, and the flavors become muted. However, this method may preserve the most nutrients. Avoid boiling sweet potatoes because they'll lose nutrients and flavor to the water.

GREENS

An integral part of any traditional Southern or soul food dinner table is the greens. While the rest of America is fawning over kale, my kin and I are still going crazy for Southern staple greens. Kale is absolutely nutritious, but no one should rely on just one dark leafy green for all their nutrients. All dark leafy greens have unique qualities, and eating a rotation of them all will help you reap the most benefits at mealtime. If you've found yourself intimidated by collard, mustard, turnip, or dandelion greens, don't worry—this book will help you fall in love with them all. Get ready!

HOW TO SLICE SWEET POTATOES

CUBED In recipes calling for cubed sweet potatoes, they should be about the size of your thumbnail, about ½ square inch (unless otherwise specified). There are many ways to cut a sweet potato, but make sure to always carefully cut with the vegetable on a flat surface, cut-side down. Also, make sure to cut your vegetables using a sharp sturdy knife to lower the risk of slipping.

WEDGES The Southern Batatas Bravas (page 78) call for the sweet potatoes to be cut into wedges. This is one of my favorite ways to cut sweet potatoes because they resemble fries and are great for eating with your hands. To cut sweet potatoes into wedges, carefully slice the potato in half. Place each half, cut-side down, on your cutting board and use your knife to slice lengthwise into 4 to 6 slices.

COLLARDS Collards are king down south. This dark leafy green most likely originated around the eastern Mediterranean region, and evidence shows that it was eaten by Greeks and Romans since at least the first century CE. Collards were introduced to the Southern states by Europeans, but it was the African slaves that made them into the dish we love today. In West Africa there had long been a tradition of preparing dark leafy greens by boiling them. This tradition made its way to the South, where slaves began to cherish this simple meal for its sheer nourishment. Food wasn't easy to come by as a slave, and nutritious collard greens could easily be grown on a small plot of land, then cooked and flavored with pork scraps. Slaves would eat their collards with cornbread that was used to sop up the pot likker—the nutritious liquid left behind in the pot. To this today, collard greens have maintained their role as an undeniable symbol of soul food.

Collard greens are high in vitamin K, calcium, potassium, cancer-fighting compounds, antioxidants, fiber, protein, vitamin A, B vitamins, iron, and so much more. Most of us are accustomed to eating stewed collards, but they can also be eaten raw in salads. My nana taught me to buy collards with smaller leaves that are bright and tender, as opposed to the large tough ones that are more mature. Though available year-round, the best collards come from your local farmers' market during your local harvest season.

TURNIPS The greens on top of the turnip plant play an important role in Southern cooking. Like collard greens, they have provided important nutrition for blacks and poor folks for hundreds of years. Also, like collards, they are usually stewed. Turnip greens are more tender than collards and have a lovely bitter flavor. Though turnip greens boast many of the same nutrients as collards, they feature characteristic cancer- and inflammation-fighting antioxidants. Look for turnip greens that are bright green and crisp.

MUSTARDS Mustard greens are from the same mustard plant as the piquant seeds used in table mustard. Like the seeds, they are bright and peppery. Mustard greens can be used in place of collards or turnip greens in stews and sautés, or all three greens can be used together.

Just 1 cup of cooked mustard greens will provide you with 922 percent of the daily value of vitamin K—important for bone health and blood clotting—even more vitamin A than collards and turnips, and almost half your daily value of vitamin C. Greens are particularly good for maintaining a healthy digestive system and gut flora, and mustards are no exception. Mustard greens look similar to turnip greens: lighter leaves with a softer stalk than collards. Look for greens that are bright in color and crisp.

DANDELIONS In addition to dark leafy greens, Southern slaves cooked with edible weeds like dandelion. This bitter weed can be found throughout the States and is often overlooked at farmers' markets and in backyards, but it is highly nutritious. Dandelion greens contain compounds that help support healthy liver detoxification. They're also high in protein; iron; calcium; vitamins A, C, and E; and B vitamins. Look for dandelion greens that are bright green or slightly red and not wilted. You can find local dandelion greens at farmers' markets in the spring.

OKRA Okra made its way to the South along with the people who originally cultivated it in West Africa. The word *okra* comes from its Igbo name, *okuru*. Known for its gelatinous seeds and heartiness, okra has long been used as a thickener in soups and gumbo throughout the South. My favorite way to enjoy okra is fried.

Okra is a great source of protein, fiber, vitamin C, B vitamins, and lots of antioxidants. Look for young tender pods when it is in season from July to September. You might even spot purple okra at your local farmers' market. It's got all the nutrition of green okra plus added benefit from phytonutrients that give it its purple hue.

SPICES

Vegetables have texture, flavor, and color on their own, but spices can take them into many different exciting directions. Down south, barbecue sauce and Creole spice blends take center stage. Barbecue sauce is tangy, sweet, and salty, the perfect condiment for grilled and smoked food. Food throughout the region may be distinct, but you'll see the same crossover spices come up again and again in recipes and spice blends: oregano, paprika, thyme, cayenne pepper, and black pepper.

Spices are loved for their flavoring ability, but they are also a good source of antioxidants and anti-inflammatory compounds. Spice blends tend to pack even more of a disease-fighting punch.

Keep your cabinet stocked with high-quality spices and spice blends so you can quickly elevate your meal. Make sure to store your spices in a cool, dry place, and keep them no longer than 6 months. Spices kept for too long will lose their flavor and health benefits. Certain spices can be pricey, so check online, in ethnic markets, and at wholesale stores for good prices.

CREOLE SEASONING

• • • • • • •

makes ½ cup

Creole cooking combines culinary traditions from African slaves (living in the United States and the Caribbean), the Spanish, Native Americans, the French, and Italians. It's colorful, it's unique, and it's got a lot of spice. Creole seasoning is used in all sorts of dishes in Louisiana and throughout the South. It's a must in Bootylicious Gumbo (page 134), Oyster Mushroom Étouffée (page 145), and Jackfruit Jambalaya (page 137).

Creole seasoning is supereasy to make with spices you've probably already got in your cabinet. Use the freshest spices for this blend to guarantee maximum flavor, freshness, and health benefit. Double the recipe if you think you'll be using it multiple times each week.

1 ½ tablespoons smoked paprika

1 tablespoon garlic powder

1 tablespoon onion powder

1 tablespoon dried thyme

1 teaspoon dried basil

1 teaspoon dried oregano or marjoram

1 teaspoon seasoned salt or sea salt (optional)

1 teaspoon freshly ground black pepper

1 teaspoon freshly ground white pepper

½ teaspoon cayenne pepper

Combine the spices in a small bowl, then transfer to a spice jar to store.

WHITE PEPPER White pepper has a distinctly different flavor that is more complex than black pepper. The spicier black pepper should not be used as a substitute.

SMOKED PAPRIKA Southern food is characteristically smoky because of the traditional use of smoked pork. Smoked paprika is a lovely spice that gives recipes that rich, smoky flavor plus sweet, spicy, or bittersweet undertones, depending on the variety. When buying smoked paprika, look for the description on the label. It'll usually describe the paprika as hot, sweet, or bittersweet. For recipes in this book I usually use either hot or bittersweet. The two can be used interchangeably, as can Hungarian and Spanish smoked paprika. The most potent smoked paprika is sold in a little metal can. Regular paprika has very little flavor and cannot be used to replace smoked paprika.

FENNEL SEEDS This European spice is perfect for giving recipes a sausage flavor without using meat. Look for whole fennel seeds, not the powder.

DRIED OREGANO Oregano is not just for pizza. This Italian herb is commonly used in Southern spice blends and cooking. It is slightly bitter, earthy, and aromatic. Sweet marjoram is often used in place of oregano.

DRIED THYME Thyme is a staple spice in Jamaican cooking, and this savory herb adds depth and richness to Southern food as well. I prefer to use dried thyme for its concentrated flavor and long shelf life.

CAYENNE PEPPER Spiciness is a cornerstone of Southern cooking, and cayenne pepper is a must-have ingredient. I always have a jar of dried cayenne next to me when I cook and a jar of Louisiana hot sauce at the table when I sit down to eat.

ONION POWDER Fresh onions are great, but onion powder concentrates and delivers that allium goodness. I wouldn't replace fresh onions with onion powder, but I use it in my Creole Seasoning (page 36) and vegan "Sweet Jesus!" Mac & "Cheese" (page 113).

BAY LEAVES I use bay leaves in stews, soups, and whenever I'm cooking a pot of beans. Stick a whole dried leaf in your pot to give the food a subtle herb essence.

VEGETABLE BOUILLON PASTE OR CUBE Buying vegetable broth is inefficient and produces too much waste, so I either make my own (see Veggie Mineral Stock on page 88) or use a vegetable bouillon paste or cube to flavor soups and stews. The replacement ratio is 4 teaspoons plus 4 cups water for every 1 quart vegetable broth. Use this stock instead of water when cooking grains, too.

NUTRITIONAL YEAST Nutritional yeast is a very flavorful powder made from inactive yeast. Its taste is nutty, cheesy, and umami (think the richness of mushrooms and soy sauce). We vegans use it to replace cheese in all sorts of recipes, and it can be added to recipes for an extra meaty quality. Though you wouldn't know from looking at it, nutritional yeast is quite nutritious. This yellowish yeast is high in protein and B vitamins. Look for it in the bulk section of your local health-focused grocery store, or find it online.

TAMARI SOY SAUCE   Soy sauce is a great ingredient to use to replace the rich umami flavor of animal products. Tamari is a more concentrated, more flavorful, and higher-quality soy sauce. Use it in place of salt in recipes.

MISO   Fermented soy products in general are great for replacing animal products. Miso, fermented soybean paste, is no exception. You'll only see it in a few of the recipes in this book, but it's worth keeping in your refrigerator. There are a few types of miso. I call for either mellow white or yellow miso. White miso has a sweet and mild flavor. Yellow miso has an earthier flavor. To be honest, I use them interchangeably, depending on what kind I have at home. Some white miso will be made with chickpeas or brown rice and can be used for the recipes. Dark miso (red or brown in color and name) will not work for the recipes in this book. It is much richer and more suitable for hearty soups with a deep umami flavor, which is not the way I use miso. White and yellow miso have a mellow flavor perfect for sauces and condiments. Miso is not as common as soy sauce, but you won't have a problem finding it at an Asian grocery store, a health food store, or online.

LIQUID SMOKE   What is barbecue sauce without smoke? Forget meat—it's the smoke that makes it barbecue. I use liquid smoke along with smoked paprika to give barbecue sauce, red beans and rice, vegan sausages, and other recipes their crucial smoky taste. Liquid smoke

is essentially collected condensation from smoking wood. The most potent liquid smokes have just two ingredients: natural smoke flavor and water. Of course, smoke in any form is a carcinogen, so use liquid smoke in moderation. It has a concentrated smoke flavor, and a very little goes a long way, making it safe for occasional use. An extra pinch of smoked paprika can be used if you don't have liquid smoke on hand.

APPLE CIDER VINEGAR   Vinegar is a must in every kitchen. Sometimes just a drop will balance a whole meal. Recipes in this cookbook use apple cider vinegar for dressings, marinades, sauces, and baking. Choose unpasteurized apple cider vinegar; it's better for you because it contains healthy bacteria and enzymes. Apple cider vinegar may aid in digestion, stabilize blood sugar levels, promote weight loss, and lower blood pressure. I also love it for its uses in personal care and around the house. Apple cider vinegar is truly a wonder ingredient!

UME PLUM VINEGAR   This fancy Japanese ingredient is like magic. It ties up any and all recipes inspired by seafood dishes. This tart and salty vinegar is a by-product of pickling *ume* plums with salt and *shiso* leaves. It's inexpensive but can be difficult to find. Look for *ume* plum vinegar at a Japanese grocery store, a health food store, or online.

DULSE & NORI   Dulse and nori sound like cute pet names, but they're actually the names of two very delicious sea vegetables. Dulse is extremely briny and perfect for use in recipes inspired by seafood dishes. Nori has a more mild flavor and can be used whenever dulse, (which is harder to find) is suggested. Sea vegetables are a good source of iodine, a crucial nutrient for thyroid functioning.

FLOURS

Biscuits, cornbread, cobbler, and pie are all important dishes in the South, and all require flour. While it is true that refined grains don't provide much nutrition, I don't think there is anything wrong with eating them in moderation. Some of the recipes in this cookbook recommend using more wholesome flours instead of all-purpose flour. Most grocery stores carry these flours nowadays. If you cannot find them, feel free to stick with what you've got.

UNBLEACHED ALL-PURPOSE FLOUR

Unbleached all-purpose flour is great for general Southern baking. The bran and germ have been removed to create a light flour with little protein, though it contains more protein than cake flour. If you are allergic to gluten, try a gluten-free flour blend to replace all-purpose flour. Note that gluten-free flour and all-purpose flour do not behave in exactly the same way, and there are many different kinds of gluten-free flour, so you might have to experiment a bit with different varieties and different amounts.

WHOLE WHEAT PASTRY FLOUR

Milled from soft white wheat, whole wheat pastry flour can replace all-purpose flour in many recipes. The bran, germ, and endosperm are intact, and despite a low protein content, baked goods will still be a little heavier with this flour. However, you'll see that I do prefer it in a few recipes.

WHOLE GRAIN OR LIGHT SPELT FLOUR

Spelt is an ancient cousin of wheat that is easier for some folks with gluten sensitivities to digest (although spelt does contain gluten). I like whole grain spelt flour for recipes that can handle a more wholesome flour. Light spelt flour can be used in place of whole wheat pastry flour.

SWEETENERS

Sugar ain't a health food, but it sure can make you feel good. It's crazy to think that before the 1700s, sugar was a rare and expensive delicacy. Today it is the single most cultivated crop in the world. Sugar is the supreme sweetener, but we'll explore a few others from the South and beyond.

CANE SUGAR Cane sugar was first brought to present-day Brazil in the 1500s, and with the exploitation of slave labor, cultivation spread throughout the Caribbean and became a booming industry in the decades and centuries to follow. As demand for sugar increased in Europe, so did the yields in the New World. Sugar was long a staple crop in the Caribbean before growers fleeing the Haitian revolution brought the cultivation to Louisiana in the late 1700s, which became, and still remains, the biggest sugar producer in the United States.

The most common type of sugar is white granulated sugar, which has gone through maximum refining to remove the molasses and any impurities, leaving pure sweet crystals. Brown sugar is also common and frequently used in

Southern cooking. It is produced by adding molasses back into refined white sugar. Raw sugar and other less refined cane sugar varieties have become popular in the last decade, but they aren't much healthier than refined white sugar. The type of sugar you should use depends most on the recipe and the flavor and texture you're seeking.

Is White Sugar Vegan? Most white sugar is processed with animal bone char to filter out impurities and remaining minerals from the product. In the end the processed sugar does not contain any bone char, but it is used in the process. Whether that counts as vegan or not is up to you. I prefer to support brands that do not use animal bone char when filtering their sugar.

MOLASSES Unlike refined sugar, molasses has nutritional value. Molasses is created by boiling freshly pressed cane juice and allowing the sugar to crystallize. The third boiling of cane juice produces blackstrap molasses, which boasts impressive amounts of iron, magnesium, calcium, and vitamin B_6. It's used for its deep, rich flavor in savory sauces and baking.

COCONUT SUGAR Made from the sap of coconut palm flowers, coconut sugar can be purchased as a thick liquid or dried and granulated. It has a lower glycemic index than cane sugar, but it should still be eaten in moderation. Coconut sugar is a great replacement for brown, turbinado, and other less processed sugars. It has a mildly floral and coconut-y flavor.

SORGHUM SYRUP In the mid-1800s, sorghum syrup became the sweetener of choice to balance the demand for cane sugar imports from the Caribbean and other parts of the Americas. Sorghum syrup comes from the sweet sorghum plant, which is a grass originally cultivated in Africa. It has a deep and complex earthy flavor, and can be used in a number of sweet and savory recipes, and even cocktails. Unless you live in the South it may be difficult to find pure sorghum syrup locally. Look for it at farmers' markets or online.

HICKORY SYRUP The Iroquois and other mid-Atlantic indigenous Americans prized hickory trees for the nutrition they provided in the form of hickory nuts and bark. Hickory syrup is made by boiling hickory bark with sugar. Native Americans would use hickory extracts for medicinal purposes, and sugar was added once Europeans arrived and the sugar industry took hold in the South. Hickory syrup is similar in taste to maple syrup but has a distinct and smoky quality. Use it wherever you'd use maple syrup. This unique sweetener can be found locally in Virginia and online.

MAPLE SYRUP Maple syrup is a distinctly Northern sweetener but can be used in a wide range of Southern vegan recipes. It's cherished for its rich, earthy sweetness, and it may sweeten everything from salad dressings to pancakes. In recipes that call for Southern sorghum syrup or hickory syrup, maple syrup may be used instead.

BAKING STAPLES

Fresh baked cornbread, cakes, and pies are the cornerstone of Southern cooking. There's no need to rely on animal products to produce sweet treats; there are plenty of plant-based ingredients to do the job.

APPLE CIDER VINEGAR Vinegar is truly a wonder food. In baking, apple cider vinegar and white vinegar produce a chemical reaction with baking powder and baking soda, resulting in light and fluffy baked goods. How? Baking soda reacts with acids to produce bubbles, which in baking help dough to rise and have structure. Baking powder is a combination of baking soda, cream of tartar, and cornstarch (or other stabilizer). It also reacts with acids, but not until it touches liquid. Apple cider vinegar and white vinegar can be used interchangeably in recipes, but I recommend keeping both in your cupboard at all times.

GROUND FLAXSEED MEAL A gelatinous mixture of ground flaxseed meal and water can be used to replace eggs in baking. The role of eggs in baked goods is to help hold ingredients together and provide structure for baking batter. Flax "eggs" can do just that. Apple cider vinegar and baking soda can also be used to give batter structure, so I don't always use flaxseed in baking. However, flaxseed comes in handy when making pancakes, waffles, muffins, and quick breads. I recommend purchasing whole flaxseeds and grinding them at home in a spice grinder. Not only is this less expensive than buying preground flax, but grinding a small amount at a time will also allow it to stay fresh longer. Flax contains oils that go rancid quickly, so store ground flaxseeds in the refrigerator or freezer. Both golden and brown flaxseeds can be used.

NONDAIRY MILK Nondairy milk is a perfect replacement for cow's milk in all recipes. Like animal's milk, it gives the batter moisture, structure, and flavor. In vegan baking, it is important to use a nondairy milk with a significant amount of richness and protein to help support the batter. I prefer to use plain unsweetened soy milk made with just soybeans and water. Almond, cashew, macadamia nut, and coconut milk are all great, too. Note that there are at least three types of coconut milk: full-fat canned, light canned, and drinking milk. The first two are for culinary use. I never use the light canned variety. In recipes that call for coconut milk, I am referring to the full-fat canned kind. Drinking coconut milk can be used to replace soy milk in baked goods as long as it is plain and unsweetened.

VEGAN BUTTER Some sort of fat is required for all great baking, and vegan butter is a terrific substitute for animal fat. Vegan butter should not be confused with margarine. Unlike trans-fat-laden margarine, vegan butter is made with nonhydrogenated plant oils. It gives a remarkably similar taste to baked goods that call for butter and can be used to produce the perfect flaky piecrust and biscuits.

Coconut oil can often be used in place of vegan butter, though it may lack the leavening and moistening power in some recipes.

BREAKFAST

· · · · · · · · · · · · · · · ·

MY FONDEST MEMORIES ARE OF SOUL FOOD breakfasts with my nana. Every Sunday I would wake up to the sound of gospel music and the smell of fluffy pancakes and home fries in the skillet wafting through the house. Since my childhood, breakfast has always been my favorite meal, so I strive to make it great, even on weekdays.

Vegan ingredients can be used to turn Southern standbys into nourishing breakfasts delicious enough to pull the deepest sleeper out of bed. I've updated some of these recipes using my favorite ingredient, sweet potato, to give them more flavor and nutrition. It's impossible for me to choose a favorite among the Fluffy Sweet Potato Biscuits (page 46), Sweet Potato Pancakes (page 52), and Sweet Potato–Pecan Cinnamon Rolls (page 65).

There are also plenty of savory breakfast options to choose from. For the ultimate Southern experience don't miss the creamy Low Country Grits (page 60), which are made with homemade vegan sausage and sautéed vegetables in a rich tomato-based broth.

CINNAMON-HONEE *butter*

• • • • • • •

makes 1 cup

Life is so much sweeter with creamy golden Honee Butter. I don't want to cause unnecessary harm to animals, so I avoid bee products, including honey. Luckily there are vegan honey alternatives. This creamy spread can be used with the Fluffy Sweet Potato Biscuits (page 46), Sweet Potato Pancakes (page 52), and the Sorghum Cornmeal Waffles (page 53). Look for Bee Free Honee online or at health-friendly grocery stores. If you cannot find it, you can substitute maple syrup, agave, or sorghum syrup instead, in the same quantity.

¾ cup vegan butter, at room temperature

2 tablespoons Bee Free Honee or other vegan liquid sweetener, plus more to taste

1 teaspoon ground cinnamon

⅛ teaspoon sea salt

1. In a medium bowl, beat the vegan butter with a hand mixer on medium speed. If you prefer, use a standing mixer. While beating, pour in the Bee Free Honee, cinnamon, and salt. Continue to beat until the ingredients have combined and the vegan butter is light and airy. This should take about 2 minutes. Taste and add more sweetener if desired. Serve at room temperature.

2. Store the Honee Butter in an airtight container in the refrigerator for up to 7 days.

FLUFFY SWEET POTATO *biscuits*

• • • • • • • •

makes 9 biscuits

You cannot have a proper Southern or soul food breakfast without flaky warm biscuits right out of the oven. These sweet potato biscuits are a delicious and healthier twist on the classic, and they don't sacrifice any of the buttery goodness of Granny's biscuits. Serve these sweet potato biscuits with Cinnamon-Honee Butter (page 45), or as a biscuit sandwich with Smoky White Bean Sausage (page 59) and Tempeh Bacon (page 63).

Making these biscuits with a food processor is a lot easier. However, if you don't have one you can still create amazing vegan biscuits. Combine the dry ingredients in a bowl with a whisk. Use a fork or—even better—a pastry cutter to cut the cold "butter" or oil into the flour, and use your hands or a wooden spoon to stir in the sweet potato mixture.

¾ cup mashed sweet potato (from ¾ baked medium sweet potato)

1 teaspoon apple cider vinegar

⅓ cup plain unsweetened soy milk or other nondairy milk

1 ½ cups whole wheat pastry flour, plus more for dusting

2 tablespoons cane sugar or coconut sugar

1 tablespoon baking powder

½ to 1 teaspoon sea salt

5 tablespoons very cold vegan butter

1. Preheat the oven to 425°F. Line a baking sheet with parchment paper and set aside.

2. In a small bowl, stir together the sweet potato, vinegar, and soy milk and set aside.

3. Place the flour, sugar, baking powder, and sea salt in a food processor and pulse to combine. Add the vegan butter and pulse until you have a coarse meal. Add the sweet potato mixture and pulse a couple times to fully combine.

4. Generously flour a clean work surface and transfer the dough onto the prepared work space. The dough will probably be fairly wet, so use the flour on the counter to help make it more manageable. Add a little more flour to the dough if needed.

5. Fold the dough over a couple of times, then pat the dough to about ½ inch thick. Cut the dough into biscuits using a biscuit cutter, a large cookie cutter (if you want fun shapes), or a wide-rimmed glass. Transfer the cut biscuits onto the prepared baking sheet.

6. Bake for 12 minutes, or until the top is golden brown. Enjoy immediately with Cinnamon-Honee Butter or sorghum syrup.

7. Store the biscuits in an airtight container at room temperature for up to 3 days.

PECAN— SWEET POTATO *granola*

• • • • • • •

makes about 4 cups

This recipe combines a few of my favorite foods into one sweet, crunchy, satisfying breakfast or snack. I love eating this fiber-rich granola with vegan coconut yogurt. It sure isn't a Southern dish, but the pecans and sweet potato certainly bring it down home!

NOTE: To shred a sweet potato, peel 1 small sweet potato and use a handheld or box grater (using the smallest hole) to shred about ½ cup. Save the leftover sweet potato to use in another recipe.

1 cup chopped pecans

2 cups old-fashioned oats

½ cup shredded peeled sweet potato (see Note)

¼ cup packed light brown sugar

1 teaspoon ground cinnamon

½ teaspoon salt

2 tablespoons pure maple syrup or agave

2 tablespoons canola oil

1 teaspoon pure vanilla extract

1. Preheat the oven to 300°F. Line a baking sheet with parchment paper and keep nearby.

2. In a large bowl, stir together all the ingredients until well combined. Spread the granola evenly in a very thin layer on the prepared baking sheet.

3. Bake for 20 minutes, until you can smell the toasting sugar and pecans. Remove from the oven and give it a stir, then spread it evenly again. Bake another 15 minutes, until the pecans are a rich brown (but not burnt). Let it cool and crisp up completely before serving.

4. Store the granola in an airtight container at room temperature for up to 4 weeks.

CHIVE & CHEDDAR *drop* BISCUITS

• • • • • • •

makes 6 biscuits

Drop biscuits are an easy and delicious alternative to cut biscuits. Savory biscuits are often underappreciated, so I was excited to create this recipe using chives and vegan cheddar. Serve these fluffy and moist biscuits along with your regular breakfast or brunch items, or enjoy them with lunch or dinner.

½ cup plain unsweetened soy milk or other nondairy milk

2 teaspoons apple cider vinegar or white vinegar

1 cup unbleached all-purpose flour

1 teaspoon sugar

1 teaspoon salt

½ teaspoon baking powder

¼ cup melted vegan butter

¼ cup minced fresh chives

¼ cup vegan cheddar

1. Preheat the oven to 450°F. Line a baking sheet with parchment paper and set aside.

2. In a small bowl, combine the soy milk and vinegar and let it curdle for at least 5 minutes while you work with the other ingredients.

3. In a medium bowl, whisk together the flour, sugar, salt, and baking powder. Gently stir in the melted vegan butter and curdled soy milk until just combined, then fold in the chives and vegan cheddar.

4. Use an ice cream scoop to drop about 3 tablespoons batter onto the baking sheet for each biscuit. There should be at least 2 inches between the biscuits.

5. Bake for 15 minutes, until the tops begin to turn golden. To keep them fresh and warm, place the biscuits in a bowl lined and covered with a clean cotton kitchen towel. Serve with Sweet Potato Skillet Home Fries (page 58) and Crispy Eggplant Bacon (page 55).

6. Store the biscuits in an airtight container at room temperature for up to 2 days. However, they're best right out of the oven.

CRISPY
EGGPLANT
BACON,
page 55

PEACH COBBLER
BREAKFAST MUFFINS,
page 54

SWEET POTATO
PANCAKES, page 52

SORGHUM CORNMEAL
WAFFLES, page 53

SWEET POTATO *pancakes*

• • • • • • • •

makes 6 to 8 pancakes

I've made a lot of pancakes in my life, and these are my favorite, rivaling the buttery, soulful pancakes my nana would make me for breakfast on Saturday and Sunday along with Sweet Potato Skillet Home Fries (page 58). These pancakes, with the rich flavor of sweet potato and the buttery, crispy edges that only a good cast-iron skillet can bless a pancake with, conjure all the fluffy comfort of my childhood. Top them with pure maple syrup or sorghum syrup and add a generous helping of Tempeh Bacon (page 63), and you've got yourself a royal Southern breakfast. To make these pancakes gluten-free, replace the spelt flour with half oat flour and half buckwheat or teff flour.

2 tablespoons ground flaxseed meal

1 ½ cups spelt flour

⅓ cup unpacked light brown sugar or coconut sugar

2 teaspoons ground cinnamon

1 teaspoon baking powder

½ teaspoon baking soda

½ teaspoon salt

¼ teaspoon freshly grated nutmeg

1 ½ cups plain unsweetened soy milk or other nondairy milk

1 teaspoon apple cider vinegar or white vinegar

1 teaspoon pure vanilla extract

¼ cup plus 2 tablespoons mashed sweet potato (from about ½ baked medium sweet potato)

2 tablespoons melted vegan butter or coconut oil, plus more for frying

Maple syrup
Tempeh Bacon (page 63)
Confectioners' sugar (optional)

1. In a large bowl, stir together the flaxseed meal and ¼ cup water. Set it aside to thicken for at least 3 minutes.

2. Meanwhile, in another large bowl, whisk together the flour, sugar, cinnamon, baking powder, baking soda, salt, and nutmeg.

3. Add the soy milk, vinegar, vanilla, sweet potato, and vegan butter to the bowl with the flaxseed meal mixture and whisk well to combine. Pour the wet ingredients into the dry ingredients and whisk until just combined. Do not overmix.

4. In a large skillet, melt 1 to 2 tablespoons vegan butter over medium heat. Ladle some batter (about ½ cup) into the skillet and fill the skillet with as many pancakes as you can comfortably fit. Cook on medium-low heat for about 3 minutes. When the centers of the pancakes start to bubble, flip and cook for another 3 minutes. Place the cooked pancakes on a clean plate, which you can keep warm in the oven at its lowest setting. Repeat with the remaining batter.

5. Top the pancakes with maple syrup and serve with strips of tempeh bacon. Sprinkle with confectioners' sugar, if desired.

SORGHUM *cornmeal* WAFFLES

· · · · · · · ·

makes **6 waffles**

Two words: Waffle House. That place was one of my first loves. These Sorghum Cornmeal Waffles are not like the waffles the Waffle House is famous for, but it was at that Southern institution that I developed my love for all waffles. Cornmeal is a Southern and soul food staple and adds great texture and depth to these waffles. Sorghum and cornmeal go together like white on rice, so there you have it. As a Southerner, I prefer to use a traditional waffle iron (with the little squares), but feel free to use whatever kind you have. If you use a Belgian waffle iron or make pancakes with the batter, add ¼ cup more soy milk to thin it out.

1 tablespoon ground flaxseed meal

¾ cup whole wheat pastry flour or unbleached all-purpose flour

½ cup fine-ground yellow cornmeal

1 teaspoon baking powder

½ teaspoon baking soda

¼ teaspoon salt

1 cup plain unsweetened soy milk or other nondairy milk

2 tablespoons melted vegan butter

1 tablespoon sorghum syrup or pure maple syrup, plus more for serving

Natural cooking oil spray, for the waffle iron

1. Preheat your waffle iron.

2. In a large bowl, combine the ground flaxseed meal and 2 tablespoons water. Set it aside to thicken for at least 3 minutes.

3. Meanwhile, in another large bowl, whisk together the flour, cornmeal, baking powder, baking soda, and salt.

4. Add the soy milk, vegan butter, and sorghum syrup to the bowl with the flaxseed meal mixture and whisk well to combine. Pour the wet ingredients into the dry ingredients and gently whisk together until just combined. Do not overmix.

5. Spray the waffle iron with the cooking oil spray and ladle about ½ cup of batter into the center. Use a spatula to quickly spread the batter. Close the iron and cook until your waffle iron indicator turns green. Place the cooked waffles on a baking sheet, which you can keep warm in the oven at its lowest setting. Repeat with the remaining batter.

6. Serve with sorghum syrup. Fresh fruit is a nice accompaniment.

PEACH COBBLER *breakfast* MUFFINS

• • • • • • • •

makes 12 muffins

A moist and hearty muffin always makes a delicious breakfast. No matter the time of year, these muffins remind me of summer. If you're making them in late summer—aka peach season—use fresh ripe peaches. If you're yearning for some Southern comfort at any other time of year, use frozen peaches or unsweetened peach preserves. The muffins will stay fresh for up to 2 days in an airtight container, or up to a month in the freezer.

CRUMBLE TOPPING

2 tablespoons spelt flour

2 tablespoons coconut sugar

¼ cup chopped pecans or walnuts

¼ teaspoon ground cardamom

1 tablespoon melted coconut or grapeseed oil

1 tablespoon ground flaxseed meal

1½ cups spelt flour

¼ cup coconut sugar or cane sugar

1 tablespoon baking powder

1 teaspoon ground cinnamon

½ teaspoon ground cardamom

½ teaspoon salt

¾ cup plain unsweetened soy milk or other nondairy milk

¼ cup melted coconut or grapeseed oil

1 teaspoon apple cider vinegar

1 teaspoon pure vanilla extract

1 ripe medium peach, halved, pitted, and chopped, or ¾ cup thawed frozen peaches, chopped

1. Preheat the oven to 350F°. Line the cups of a muffin pan and set aside.

2. Make the topping: In a small bowl, mix together the flour, sugar, pecans, cardamom, and oil until well combined. Set aside until ready to use.

3. In a large bowl, stir together the flaxseed meal and 2 tablespoons water. Set it aside to thicken for at least 3 minutes.

4. In another large bowl, whisk together the flour, sugar, baking powder, cinnamon, cardamom, and salt.

5. Add the soy milk, oil, vinegar, and vanilla to the bowl with the flaxseed meal mixture and whisk well to combine. Pour the wet mixture into the dry and stir together until just combined. Do not overmix. Gently fold the chopped peaches into the batter.

6. Spoon the batter into the muffin cups, filling each one halfway. Sprinkle about 1 tablespoon of the topping on each muffin. Bake for 30 minutes, or until a toothpick comes out clean.

CRISPY EGGPLANT *bacon*

• • • • • • •

serves 4

A good Southern breakfast just ain't complete without bacon. This eggplant "bacon" has all the smokiness and saltiness of the real stuff but without the animal cruelty and heart-clogging cholesterol. Eggplant may not seem like a likely bacon substitute, but it soaks up the seasoning and crisps up like magic.

¼ cup soy sauce

2 teaspoons pure maple syrup or hickory syrup

1 teaspoon liquid smoke

1 teaspoon smoked paprika

1 small Italian eggplant, peeled and thinly sliced into ⅛-inch-thick and 1-inch-wide strips

1. Preheat the oven to 300°F. Line a baking sheet with parchment paper and keep nearby.

2. In a medium bowl, stir together the soy sauce, maple syrup, liquid smoke, and paprika. Dip the strips of eggplant into the mixture and gently massage. Place the eggplant strips on the prepared baking sheet. Bake for about 20 minutes, or until crispy.

SWEET POTATO SKILLET
HOME FRIES, page 58

LOW COUNTRY GRITS,
page 60

SMOKY WHITE BEAN
SAUSAGE, page 59

SWEET POTATO *skillet* HOME FRIES

. . . .

serves **4 to 6**

I'll never forget the love and attention my nana would put into peeling and slicing potatoes for home fries every Saturday morning. She'd hold each potato in her left hand as she sliced them into thin disks with her right. There was something so artistic and enchanting about that. This recipe is a take on Nana's breakfast classic. It utilizes bright orange sweet potatoes to increase the nutrient value—sweet potatoes are loaded with beta-carotene—and fiber content. I especially like to make this dish with a mix of orange and white sweet potatoes.

5 to 6 tablespoons coconut oil

1 medium yellow onion, diced

1 large red bell pepper, diced

2 teaspoons sea salt, or to taste

3 sweet potatoes, peeled and cut into ½-inch cubes

2 teaspoons sweet smoked paprika

1 teaspoon fennel seeds

1 teaspoon red chili flakes

1 teaspoon freshly ground black pepper

¼ cup chopped fresh parsley

1. In a large skillet, melt 2 tablespoons of the oil over medium heat. Add the onion, bell pepper, and 1 teaspoon of the salt. Sauté until the onion is translucent, about 3 minutes. Transfer the onion and bell pepper to a small bowl and set aside.

2. In the same skillet, melt the remaining oil over medium-high heat. Add the sweet potatoes and the remaining teaspoon salt. Fry for 2 minutes. Cover the skillet and continue to cook for 8 minutes, stirring halfway through. Remove the lid and let the potatoes cook a little longer, until they are tender.

3. Stir in the cooked onion and bell pepper, paprika, fennel seeds, red chili flakes, and pepper. Taste for seasoning and add more salt if desired. Stir in the parsley and serve the home fries hot.

SMOKY WHITE BEAN
sausage

· · · · · · · ·

**makes 4 large sausages
or 8 small breakfast sausages**

I hope you'll be revisiting this recipe over and over. Inspired by an Isa Chandra Moskowitz recipe, these sausages deliver great flavor and meaty texture. One of the prime flavors of the South is smoke. We always seem to have the smoker fired up and add smoked foods to many dishes. I've included these in the breakfast section because they can be served with any one of the morning recipes. You'll also see them pop up in a few other recipes in this book because they're so incredibly versatile. Lucky for us all, they're also a cinch to make.

Make sure your beans are well cooked until very soft (see page 125). Hard beans will be too difficult to mash. Whatever you do with these perfect sausages—reheat, grill, sauté—they retain their great texture. They will keep fresh for up to 7 days in the refrigerator.

1 cup cooked cannellini beans (see page 125) or a little less than half a 15-ounce can

¼ cup Veggie Mineral Stock (page 88) or ¼ cup water plus ¼ vegetable bouillon cube

2 tablespoons pure maple syrup

1 ½ tablespoons soy sauce

1 tablespoon olive oil

1 tablespoon white miso

2 teaspoons smoked paprika

1 teaspoon dried thyme

1 teaspoon fennel seeds

1 teaspoon red chili flakes

1 teaspoon freshly ground black pepper

¼ cup minced yellow or red onion

¼ cup diced peeled Yukon Gold potato

¾ cup vital wheat gluten

2 tablespoons nutritional yeast

1 tablespoon potato starch

1. Place the beans in a large bowl and mash with a fork until mostly creamy; the texture should be a bit chunky. Add the remaining ingredients and stir until thoroughly combined. You may need to use your hands to form the batter into a ball, as the batter will be very thick.

2. Place the ball of batter onto a cutting board and cut it into 4 sections. Then use your hands to form each section into a sausage shape. Make sure to pack the batter tightly as you shape it. Alternatively, you can halve each quarter and shape the batter into 8 small breakfast links. Wrap each sausage tightly in a square-foot sheet of aluminum foil, twisting the ends to seal the sausage inside.

3. Set a steaming basket over 1 to 2 inches of boiling water, add the sausages, tightly cover, and steam for 45 minutes. Replenish the water level when necessary.

4. Remove the sausages from the heat and let cool until safe to handle. Place them, still wrapped in foil, in the refrigerator to firm for at least 3 hours or up to overnight.

5. When you're ready to use the sausages, slice them and pan-fry to reheat them before serving or add sausages directly into other recipes that call for vegan sausage.

LOW COUNTRY GRITS

• • • • • • •

serves 4

Grits are one of the ultimate Southern staples. If you've never tried them, this is a great introduction. Topped with a tomato-based stew, this dish is ideal for any savory breakfast fan. Grits, like most Southern foods, are made differently throughout the region. Some like them savory; others prefer them sweet. This version was inspired by the flavors of the Low Country, a coastal region on South Carolina's and Georgia's Sea Islands, where seafood is eaten in abundance. These grits get their "seafood" essence from zucchini and artichoke hearts for texture, and from Old Bay seasoning and *ume* plum vinegar for flavor.

1 tablespoon grapeseed or olive oil

2 garlic cloves, minced

6 to 8 scallions (white and light green parts), chopped, green parts reserved for garnish

½ medium jalapeño pepper, seeded and minced

1 (14-ounce) can diced tomatoes or 2 large hothouse tomatoes, diced (about 1½ cups)

1 small zucchini, halved and thinly sliced

1 (8-ounce) jar marinated artichoke hearts, drained

½ cup thawed frozen corn

1 Creole Red Bean Sausage (page 99) or Smoky White Bean Sausage (page 59), sliced about ¼ inch thick

2 teaspoons Old Bay seasoning

1 teaspoon Creole Seasoning (page 36)

1½ teaspoons tamari soy sauce

1 teaspoon *ume* plum vinegar

¼ cup chopped fresh parsley

4 cups plain unsweetened soy milk or other nondairy milk

1 tablespoon vegan butter or olive oil

1 teaspoon salt

1 teaspoon freshly ground black pepper

1 cup old-fashioned grits

2 tablespoons nutritional yeast (optional)

1. In a large skillet, heat the oil over medium heat. Sauté the garlic, scallion whites, and jalapeño, about 3 minutes. Add the tomatoes, zucchini, artichoke hearts, corn, sausage, and 1 cup water and bring to a simmer for about 5 minutes. Add the seasonings and tamari. On low heat simmer until the zucchini is tender, about 10 minutes. Stir in the vinegar and parsley. There should be ample broth. Reduce the heat to its lowest setting to keep them warm.

2. Meanwhile, in a medium saucepan over medium-high heat, bring the soy milk to a low boil. Add the butter, salt, and pepper, then stir in the grits.

3. Reduce the heat to low and continue to stir for 20 to 30 minutes, until creamy. If the grits look dry, stir in water—2 tablespoons at a time. Once creamy, stir in the nutritional yeast.

4. Spoon the grits and vegetable sauté into bowls. Garnish with nutritional yeast and scallion greens.

CREAMY *teff* PORRIDGE

● ● ● ● ● ● ●

serves 2

For the ultimate stick-to-your-ribs breakfast, I make this rich and satisfying porridge. Teff is an ancient grain from Ethiopia. You may recognize it from the country's notable cuisine—teff flour is used to make the signature Ethiopian bread, *injera*. Look for whole grain teff, not flour, to make this recipe. The tiny grain is loaded with fiber, protein, magnesium, potassium, and so much more. I enjoy this porridge with nuts and fruit to add even more flavor and nutrition.

¾ cup teff grain

½ to 1 cup plain unsweetened soy milk or other nondairy milk

1 teaspoon ground cinnamon

2 tablespoons pure maple syrup, or to taste

½ cup chopped pecans or walnuts, for serving

¼ cup raisins, chopped dates, chopped apricots, or other dried fruit, for serving

1 cup fresh seasonal fruit, for serving

1. In a medium saucepan over medium heat, lightly toast the teff grains for about 30 seconds. Add 2¼ cups water, stir, and raise the heat to high to bring to a boil. Reduce the heat to medium-low and simmer for 10 minutes, stirring occasionally to prevent the teff from sticking.

2. Once the teff has thickened, stir in the soy milk, depending on how thick or thin you want it. Partly cover the pan and continue simmering for another 10 minutes. Stir in the cinnamon and maple syrup, then remove from the heat. Taste and add more cinnamon or syrup if desired.

3. Serve in a bowl and top with chopped nuts, dried fruit, and fresh fruit.

TEMPEH
bacon

• • • • • • • •

serves 4

There are so many ways to make vegan bacon, but along with Crispy Eggplant Bacon (page 55), this is my favorite method. The longer you marinate the tempeh, the better it takes on the seasoning's rich, complex flavors. Not only is tempeh delicious, but it's also full of fiber and protein—the perfect breakfast nutrients.

¼ cup soy sauce

¼ cup pure maple syrup

2 tablespoons grapeseed or olive oil

1 tablespoon liquid smoke

1 teaspoon smoked paprika

1 (8-ounce) package tempeh, halved and thinly sliced lengthwise into ¼-inch strips

1. Place the soy sauce, maple syrup, oil, liquid smoke, and paprika in a glass jar with a tight-fitting lid. Secure the lid and shake vigorously to combine and emulsify the ingredients.

2. Place the tempeh in a shallow baking dish and cover with the marinade. Marinate in the refrigerator for at least 4 hours or up to overnight.

3. Preheat the oven to 375°F. Line a baking sheet with parchment paper and keep nearby.

4. Remove the tempeh from the refrigerator. Place the tempeh strips in a single layer on the prepared baking sheet. Bake for 20 minutes, or until crispy around the edges.

SWEET POTATO– *pecan* CINNAMON ROLLS

• • • • • • • •

makes 12 rolls

Some people categorize cinnamon rolls as dessert, but I've only ever known them as a special breakfast treat. There's nothing like a warm freshly baked cinnamon roll right out of the oven with gooey sweet potato cream cheese icing drizzled on top. If you've never made cinnamon rolls, you'll love how fun and easy these are to make. My favorite part is rolling the sweet potato dough around the pecan and cinnamon filling.

1 cup plain unsweetened soy milk or other nondairy milk

¼ cup vegan butter

1 cup mashed sweet potato (from 1 baked medium sweet potato)

3 cups unbleached all-purpose flour, plus more for dusting

¼ cup granulated sugar

1 (¼-ounce) package (2¼ teaspoons) active dry yeast

½ teaspoon salt

½ teaspoon grapeseed oil

FILLING

½ cup brown sugar, coconut sugar, or a mix of the two

½ tablespoon ground cinnamon

¾ cup toasted pecans (see Note on page 164)

⅓ cup vegan butter

SWEET POTATO CREAM CHEESE FROSTING

½ cup vegan cream cheese

½ cup confectioners' sugar

¼ cup mashed sweet potato (from ¼ baked medium sweet potato)

½ teaspoon pure vanilla extract

1. In a small saucepan, warm the soy milk and vegan butter over medium heat until the vegan butter has melted. Do not boil it. Remove from the heat and stir in the mashed sweet potato.

2. In a large bowl, mix together the flour, granulated sugar, yeast, and salt. Pour the liquid ingredients into the dry and use a wooden spoon to combine. Once it gets too difficult to stir, use your hands to combine the ingredients.

3. Flour a clean work surface and transfer the dough onto the prepared work space. Knead it until you've got a smooth dough ball. Lightly oil a large bowl. Place the dough ball in it, cover with plastic wrap or a kitchen towel, and let it rise for 1 hour. The dough should double in size.

recipe continues

4. Make the filling: In a small bowl, combine the brown sugar and cinnamon and set aside. Chop the pecans into small pieces and set aside. In a small saucepan, melt the vegan butter and set aside.

5. Once the dough has doubled in size, preheat the oven to 375°F.

6. Press the air out of the dough, then transfer it back onto your floured work space. Roll the dough until it is about ¼ inch thick. You should end up with a roughly rectangular oval, about 12 × 16 inches.

7. Brush the dough with the melted butter, sprinkle with the cinnamon-sugar mix, and then top with the chopped pecans. Fold the short side of the dough over and roll tightly until you have a log. Carefully cut the log into twelve 1-inch slices. Grease a large skillet or a 10 × 10-inch baking dish and place the rolls in it cut-side down. Bake for 25 minutes, or until they've expanded and turned slightly golden on the top.

8. Meanwhile, make the frosting: Place all the ingredients in a food processor or standing mixer with the whisk attachment on high and blend until creamy.

9. Remove the rolls from oven and let cool for 5 to 10 minutes. Top with the sweet potato frosting and serve immediately. They will stay fresh for up to 2 days, but they're best eaten the day you bake them.

SWEET POTATO PIE *smoothie*

. . . .

serves 2

When I'm craving the flavors of sweet potato pie for breakfast, I make this comforting smoothie. Always keep baked sweet potatoes in your refrigerator so you can make this smoothie in a pinch. Canned sweet potato will also work, but home-baked potatoes are the best choice.

2 cups plain unsweetened soy milk or other nondairy milk, plus more as needed

1 cup mashed sweet potato (from 1 baked medium sweet potato)

½ teaspoon pure vanilla extract

1 teaspoon ground cinnamon

¼ teaspoon freshly grated nutmeg

1½ tablespoons pure maple syrup or 1 pitted date

Place all the ingredients in a blender and blend until smooth. Add more nondairy milk to thin if necessary.

SALADS & SOUPS

· · · · · · · · · · · · · · · ·

MY TWO FONDEST MEMORIES OF SOUP are my nana's chicken noodle soup and the bean soups or chili my mom would send me to school with, packed in a hefty canteen. While my friends munched on cafeteria pizza and french fries, I'd savor my home-cooked creation.

As a private chef and blogger, I'm always asked to create hearty salad and soup recipes. As a vegan, I've come to see these dishes as more than sides to be served alongside a "protein." Salads and soups have as much business being enjoyed as an entrée as hearty main dishes do. They're nutrient-dense, full of protein (veggies are rich in plant-based protein), fiber-ful, and fun!

The nutritious salads and soups in this chapter prove that Southern and soul food is about more than fried foods and butter-laden sweets. At the heart of soul cooking you'll find fresh, seasonal, and local fruits and vegetables. A few of these recipes rely on new ways to prepare old favorites and can serve as an introduction to classic Southern ingredients like collards, dandelion greens, butter beans, and sweet potatoes. Mix and match these recipes to create a colorful meal packed with a wide variety of phytonutrients, texture, and flavor. One of my favorite winning combinations is the Sunflower Caesar Salad (page 76) with the Harlem Caviar: Black-eyed Pea Salad (page 85) and Southern Batatas Bravas (page 78). Of course, you should also try these salads and soups alongside this book's other sides and main dishes. How about the Rainbow Root Slaw (page 79) with Jalapeño Hush Puppies (page 104), and Bourbon BBQ Tempeh Sandwiches (page 142). Can I get an amen?

pop's TANGY GREEN BEAN SALAD

. . . .

serves 4

My dad is famous for his nutritional yeast salad dressing, which he says he learned while working at Atlanta's original vegan restaurant, Soul Veg. The stuff is so good that you could literally eat it with a spoon. Luckily for the world, he has given me permission to publish his masterpiece. Thanks, Daddy! Serve this dressing over fresh blanched green beans or salad greens, or try it with steamed, raw, grilled, or roasted veggies. If you've been craving a vegan dressing with cheesy richness and strong flavor, this one is the answer!

1 pound fresh green beans, trimmed

2 tablespoons apple cider vinegar

2 tablespoons nutritional yeast

2 tablespoons olive oil

2 tablespoons minced shallot

1 tablespoon stone-ground or Dijon mustard

1 teaspoon freshly ground black pepper

Dash of cayenne pepper

1. Set a steaming basket over 1 to 2 inches of boiling water, add the green beans, tightly cover, and steam until bright green yet tender, about 5 minutes. Transfer the beans to a serving bowl.

2. In a small bowl, whisk together the vinegar, yeast, oil, shallot, mustard, pepper, and cayenne until creamy. Toss the green beans with the dressing and serve warm or at room temperature.

BOURBON BBQ TEMPEH
SANDWICHES, page 142

COCONUT COLLARD
SALAD, page 74

COCONUT
collard
SALAD

• • • • • • • •

serves **2 to 4**

I'll never forget the time I told my
nana I was using raw collard greens
to replace a wheat tortilla in a wrap.
"I've never heard of eating raw collard
greens, Jenné," was her incredulous
response. Despite her skepticism, it
delighted me to know that collards were
having a rebirth in the raw food and
vegan communities. They're actually
quite delicious raw and, just like kale,
can be massaged to tender perfection.
This recipe is inspired by a raw coconut
collard salad I had at the Cecil, an
African Asian fusion restaurant in
Harlem. We should all definitely be
eating more raw collards, and this
recipe is the perfect way to add them to
our plate.

1 bunch of collard greens, tough stems removed and leaves
    thinly sliced into ¼-inch ribbons (see Note on page 103)
¼ cup full-fat coconut milk
2 tablespoons seasoned rice vinegar
1 tablespoon soy sauce
Pinch of cayenne pepper
¼ cup Quick-Pickled Onions (page 75)

1. Place the collard ribbons in a large salad bowl.

2. Combine the coconut milk, vinegar, soy sauce, and
cayenne in a small glass jar with a tight-fitting lid. Secure
the lid and shake vigorously until blended.

3. Pour the dressing over the collards and gently
massage into the greens. Top with the pickled onions and
serve immediately.

QUICK-PICKLED ONIONS

• • • • • • •

makes 1 16-ounce jar

Add pickled onions to almost any dish for a burst of flavor and crunch, and this recipe offers a supereasy method for pickling. I especially like to make a few jars of pickled Vidalia onions in the summer so that I can enjoy their sweet Georgia flavor for months. If you cannot find Vidalia onions, red onions are a great alternative.

1 cup apple cider vinegar

2 tablespoons sugar

1 teaspoon salt

½ teaspoon fennel seeds

1 large Vidalia or red onion, very thinly sliced

1. Combine the vinegar, sugar, salt, and fennel seeds in a 16-ounce glass jar with a tight-fitting lid. Stir well until the sugar and salt dissolve. Add the sliced onions and press them down gently to cover completely with the pickling liquid. Secure the lid and set aside on the kitchen counter to let them pickle for at least 1 hour before using.

2. Store the onions in a tightly sealed glass jar in the refrigerator for 2 weeks.

SUNFLOWER CAESAR SALAD

• • • • • • •

serves 2 to 4

Salads are supposed to be healthy, but Caesar salads are so often the furthest thing from that. My take on this American staple uses a mix of kale and romaine, plus vitamin E–rich sunflower seeds as the base of the creamy dressing. Tossed with smoky Tempeh Bacon (page 63) and Cornbread Croutons, this salad will make you crave raw greens like never before. Make sure to cut the kale into thin strips, and when adding the dressing, massage it well for the most delectable salad.

1 bunch of kale, tough stems removed and leaves sliced into ½-inch ribbons (see Note on page 103)

1 bunch of romaine lettuce, sliced into ½-inch ribbons (see Note on page 103)

2 cups Cornbread Croutons (recipe follows)

¼ to ½ recipe of Tempeh Bacon (page 63)

CAESAR DRESSING

½ cup raw sunflower seeds, soaked overnight and drained

1 garlic clove

3 tablespoons nutritional yeast

2 tablespoons capers, drained and rinsed

4 teaspoons vegan Worcestershire sauce

2 tablespoons freshly squeezed lemon juice

1 tablespoon tamari soy sauce

2 teaspoons Dijon mustard

2 teaspoons freshly ground black pepper

2 tablespoons extra-virgin olive oil

1. Place the sliced kale in a large salad bowl. Keep the romaine separate for now.

2. Make the dressing: Place the sunflower seeds, garlic, nutritional yeast, capers, vegan Worcestershire sauce, lemon juice, tamari, mustard, and pepper in a blender and add ¼ cup water. Blend until creamy, then slowly pour in the oil while the blender is still running and blend until smooth.

3. Using your clean hands, massage about half the dressing into the kale until it is tender, about 2 minutes. Add the romaine lettuce and a couple more spoonfuls of dressing and toss to coat.

4. Top with the croutons and crumble the tempeh bacon on top.

CORNBREAD CROUTONS

• • • • • • •

makes 6 cups

Add Southern flair to salads, stews, and soups by tossing in a handful of cornbread croutons. They've also become one of my favorite crunchy snacks. I tend to make these croutons when my cornbread begins to get stale. The recipe calls for fresh cornbread, but if you're using leftover cornbread that has begun to dry out, you'll need to adjust your oil and salt downward according to the amount of leftovers you're working with.

1 recipe Skillet Cornbread (page 102), cut into ½-inch cubes

3 tablespoons olive oil

2 teaspoons salt

1. Preheat the oven to 350°F. Line a baking sheet with parchment paper and keep nearby.

2. In a large bowl, toss the cubed cornbread with the oil. Arrange the cubes evenly on the prepared baking sheet and sprinkle on the salt. Toast in the oven for 25 minutes, flipping the cubes after about 15 minutes. If the croutons are not crispy after 25 minutes, stir again and toast for another 10 minutes.

southern BATATAS BRAVAS

• • • • • • •

serves **4**

I spent a semester in Madrid when I was in college and fell in love with Spanish *patatas bravas*. They remind me of Southern comfort food. Traditionally this tapa is made with starchy white potatoes and an egg-based mayonnaise, but I chose to make it my own with sweet potatoes (called *batatas* in Spanish) and vegan mayo. The result is a healthier comfort food that takes me back to my time spent living in the Spanish capital.

3 sweet potatoes, sliced into wedges (see page **34**)

2 tablespoons melted coconut oil

1 teaspoon coarse salt

½ cup vegan mayonnaise

1 garlic clove

1 tablespoon tomato paste

1 tablespoon Dijon mustard

1 teaspoon red wine vinegar

1 teaspoon freshly ground black pepper

½ teaspoon smoked paprika

2 tablespoons chopped fresh parsley, for garnish

1. Preheat the oven to 350°F. Line a baking sheet with parchment paper or a silicone mat and keep nearby.

2. In a medium bowl, toss the sweet potato wedges with the oil. Arrange the potato wedges evenly on the prepared baking sheet and sprinkle ½ teaspoon of the salt over them. Bake for 35 minutes, or until tender and crispy around the edges.

3. While the sweet potatoes bake, make the sauce. Place the vegan mayonnaise, garlic, tomato paste, mustard, vinegar, pepper, paprika, and the remaining ½ teaspoon of salt in a blender. Blend until creamy.

4. Transfer the sweet potatoes to a serving plate and top with a generous drizzle of the sauce. Garnish with fresh parsley. Serve immediately.

rainbow ROOT SLAW

• • • • • • • •

serves **4 to 6**

You can't have a Southern cookout without coleslaw, and for a really good time, make this colorful slaw. It's just as easy to make as the traditional monochromatic cabbage salad, but it's so much healthier and prettier. An easy and delicious way to improve the healthfulness of your food is to make colorful swaps, such as red cabbage for white. Vibrant colors in fruits and vegetables are an indication of the vitamins and phytonutrients that behave as antioxidants in your body. Eat your rainbow!

This recipe calls for shredded vegetables. My favorite time- and effort-saving tip is to shred them in the food processor using the large shredding blade. If you don't have this, use a box grater on its largest shredding side.

1 small head of red cabbage (about 1 pound), outer leaves and core removed, shredded

3 medium carrots, shredded (about 1½ cups)

1 large beet, peeled and shredded (about ½ cup)

¼ cup diced red or white onion

½ cup vegan mayonnaise

1 tablespoon Dijon mustard

1 tablespoon freshly squeezed lemon juice

1 tablespoon apple cider vinegar

2 teaspoons pure maple syrup or agave nectar

1 teaspoon salt

1 teaspoon freshly ground black pepper

½ teaspoon red chili flakes

1. In a large salad bowl, toss together the shredded cabbage, carrots, and beet.

2. In a small bowl, whisk together the onion, vegan mayonnaise, mustard, lemon juice, vinegar, maple syrup, salt, pepper, and red chili flakes until creamy. Pour the dressing over the slaw and toss to coat well. Let it marinate in the refrigerator at least 1 hour before serving.

MISO PEACHY ARUGULA
SALAD, page 83

PURPLE AND WHITE
POTATO SALAD, page 82

GEORGIA WATERMELON
& PEACH SALAD, page 84

PURPLE AND WHITE POTATO SALAD

• • • • • • •

serves **4**

Potato salad became my jam after I became vegan. Growing up, I wouldn't touch the stuff with a ten-foot pole—I had a strong aversion to anything white and creamy—but that all changed when I tasted potato salad made with fresh and clean vegan mayonnaise. This easy-to-make recipe gets its name from the colors of the potatoes. For the perfect potato salad, be careful not to overcook your potatoes, and be sure to let the potato salad sit in the refrigerator for at least 2 hours (better still, overnight) before serving. If you cannot find *ume* plum vinegar, use old-fashioned relish instead.

3 small unpeeled Yukon Gold potatoes

3 small unpeeled purple potatoes

½ cup vegan mayonnaise

3 tablespoons minced shallots

3 tablespoons minced fresh dill

2 tablespoons *ume* plum vinegar

2 teaspoons Dijon mustard

1 ½ teaspoons sea salt, or to taste

1. In a large pot, bring 8 cups of water to a boil. Add the potatoes and reduce the heat to a simmer. Boil the potatoes for about 20 minutes, or until tender but not mushy.

2. Drain the potatoes in a colander. When cool enough to handle, remove the potato skins and cut the potatoes into ½-inch cubes. Place the potatoes in a large bowl.

3. In a small bowl, whisk together the vegan mayonnaise, shallots, dill, vinegar, mustard, and salt until creamy. Pour the dressing over the potatoes and stir gently but well to coat. Taste for seasoning and add more salt if desired. Place the potato salad in the refrigerator and marinate for at least 2 hours and up to overnight before serving.

NUTRITION STAPLE: Did you know that dill is an incredibly healthy herb? It is considered a chemoprotective food because it contains compounds that neutralize free carcinogens that come from cigarette smoke and grills. This will really come in handy if you plan to take this potato salad to an omnivore cookout where your friends are grilling meat. Dill also has antibacterial properties, which will help your potato salad stay fresh for longer.

MISO PEACHY ARUGULA *salad*

• • • • • • •

serves **4**

When peaches are in abundance during mid- to late summer, I do my best to use them in as many dishes as possible. Maybe it's because I'm a Georgia Peach, maybe it's because they're outrageously juicy, or maybe it's because of their incredible versatility, but peaches are one of my favorite fruits. This dressing was inspired by the miso-ginger salad dressing that got me to eat a salad for the first time as a teenager. I love slightly sweet dressings, so the addition of peach is a no-brainer. Miso is a Japanese fermented soybean paste. It's got a lot of rich umami flavor that blends well with the peach and citrus in the dressing. Unfortunately, there is no good substitute for miso. If you cannot get your hands on it, use 1 teaspoon Dijon mustard in place of the miso for a different take.

6 cups arugula

8 ounces sugar snap peas, strings removed (about ½ cup)

2 radishes, thinly sliced

1 ½ ripe medium peaches, halved, pitted, and diced

2 tablespoons white miso

3 teaspoons apple cider vinegar, plus more to taste

½ teaspoon freshly ground black pepper

¼ cup olive oil

½ cup Hot Pepper Pecans (page 87), optional

½ ripe medium peach, halved, pitted, and sliced ¼ inch thick

1. In a large salad bowl, toss together the arugula, sugar snaps, and sliced radishes and set aside.

2. Place the diced peaches in a blender along with the miso, vinegar, and pepper. Blend until creamy, then slowly pour in the oil while the blender is still running and blend until smooth. Taste for seasoning and add more vinegar if desired. Pour the dressing over the vegetables and toss well. Top with the pecans, if desired, and the sliced peaches and serve.

GEORGIA
watermelon & peach
SALAD

• • • • • • • •

serves **2 to 4**

This recipe is inspired by my stepmother, Regina, who is from Savannah. She was the first person I ever saw eat watermelon with salt. When I was a kid I wouldn't dare try it, but funnily enough, I love it today, and it's made me realize the versatility of watermelon. This Georgia Watermelon & Peach Salad makes use of two of the South's most prized crops and marries them with a savory sweet dressing. The result is a mouthwatering, delicious late-summer salad.

4 cups cubed seedless watermelon, cut into ½-inch cubes

2 ripe medium peaches, halved, pitted, and sliced ¼ inch thick

2 ripe medium tomatoes, cut into ½-inch cubes

LIME VINAIGRETTE

¼ cup olive oil

Juice of 2 limes

1 teaspoon agave, pure maple syrup, or coconut nectar

Dash of sea salt

1 handful of basil, whole leaves or leaves cut into ¼-inch ribbons (see Note on page 103)

¼ cup lightly toasted pumpkin seeds (see Note on page 164)

1. Gently toss together the watermelon, peaches, and tomatoes in a large bowl.

2. Make the vinaigrette: Place the oil, lime juice, agave, and salt in a small jar with a tight-fitting lid. Secure the lid and shake vigorously until emulsified. Drizzle about ¼ cup of the vinaigrette onto the salad and stir in the basil and half the pumpkin seeds. Just before serving, drizzle the remaining dressing onto the salad and garnish with more pumpkin seeds and whole basil leaves.

HARLEM CAVIAR: BLACK-EYED PEA *salad*

• • • • • • • •

serves 6

If I had to choose a favorite bean, it would definitely be black-eyed peas. Being a Southern girl living in the Northeast, black-eyed peas are one of the foods that most reminds me of home. This cold bean salad is ideal for warm-weather meals and can be enjoyed as a side dish or main. Serve it with Skillet Cornbread (page 102) and Coconut Collard Salad (page 74) for an absolutely satisfying yet simple meal.

3 cups cooked black-eyed peas (see page 125) or 2 (15-ounce) cans, drained and rinsed

½ cup chopped celery

¼ cup chopped red onion

1 medium red bell pepper, roasted and chopped (see Note on page 214)

1 tablespoon Dijon mustard

1 tablespoon apple cider vinegar

1 to 2 teaspoons hot sauce (depending on your spice tolerance)

1 teaspoon pure maple syrup or agave

1¼ teaspoons sea salt

1 teaspoon dried oregano

1 teaspoon dried thyme

2 tablespoons olive oil

¼ cup chopped fresh parsley

1. In a large bowl, toss together the black-eyed peas, celery, onion, and roasted bell pepper in a large bowl.

2. In a small bowl, whisk together the mustard, vinegar, hot sauce, maple syrup, salt, oregano, and thyme. Drizzle in the oil while whisking vigorously until the mixture is well blended and creamy. Pour the dressing over the black-eyed peas and stir well to combine.

3. This dish is best when made a few hours or the night before. Stir in the fresh parsley just before serving.

COOL-AS-A-CUCUMBER *salad*

• • • • • • •

serves **2 to 4**

Eating with the seasons is one of the easiest things you can do to improve your health and save money on food. I'm in awe of how Mother Nature provides us with cooling water-rich foods, like cucumber and peaches, during the warmest months of the year. Cucumbers are high in phytonutrient compounds called cucurbitacins, which have been studied for their anticancer powers. Like peaches, cucumbers are their best when they're in season, so fill up on them all through the summer months.

2 large cucumbers, peeled, seeded, and cut into ¼-inch cubes

1 ripe medium peach, halved, pitted, and cut into ¼-inch cubes

1 ripe avocado, halved, pitted, and cut into ¼-inch cubes

¼ cup minced red onion

¼ cup chopped fresh dill

1½ teaspoons apple cider vinegar, plus more to taste

1 tablespoon freshly squeezed lemon juice, plus more to taste

¾ teaspoon sea salt, plus more to taste

¼ teaspoon cayenne pepper

Place all the ingredients in a large bowl and stir gently but well to combine. Taste for seasoning and add more salt, vinegar, or lemon juice if desired.

HOT PEPPER *pecans*

· · · · · · · · ·

makes 3 cups

If you like it hot, you'll love these sweet, spicy, salty nuts. They make a healthy snack and are superdelicious sprinkled on top of salads or soups. Pecans, like all nuts, are full of heart-healthy fat. Unlike the fat found in animal products or refined oils, the fat in nuts and seeds supports the healthy functioning of your heart, sustains your energy, and keeps you full longer. Folks who eat nuts every day tend to have a healthier body weight, so skip the potato chips and snack on these instead. As you know, I'm tragically allergic to peanuts, but if you're not, feel free to use them in place of pecans or do a mix of the two for this recipe. Just don't sneak them onto my plate.

3 tablespoons Louisiana hot sauce

3 tablespoons pure maple syrup

2½ cups raw pecans or peanuts

1 teaspoon Maldon sea salt flakes or other coarse sea salt

1. Preheat the oven to 350°F. Line a baking sheet with parchment paper and keep nearby.

2. In a medium bowl, stir together the hot sauce and maple syrup. Add the pecans and stir well to coat. Arrange the pecans evenly on the prepared baking sheet and sprinkle on the salt. Roast for 10 minutes, give the nuts a good stir, and continue roasting another 10 minutes. Remove from the oven to cool and harden. Store in an airtight container for up to 2 weeks.

VEGGIE *mineral* STOCK

• • • • • • •

makes 2½ quarts

10 cups water

8 cups assorted vegetable scraps

1. In a large stockpot, bring the water to a boil. Add the vegetable scraps, then reduce the heat to medium-low and lightly simmer for 30 minutes. Remove from the heat and let the stock cool to room temperature. Strain the stock through a fine-mesh strainer into 2 quart-size storage containers.

2. Store the stock in an airtight container in the refrigerator for up to 5 days or freeze for up to 1 month.

Few things are as grounding, wholesome, and easy to prepare as homemade vegetable stock. It's economical, too. Simply save all your clean food scraps—onion peels, carrot tops, celery bottoms, mushroom stalks, ginger peels, and so on—as you cook throughout the week. Scraps that don't work well are sandy leek roots, onion roots, and onion or garlic paper. I stash my scraps in the freezer, and once that half-gallon plastic bag is full, it's time to make stock! This soup base is loaded with vitamins and minerals that are stored in the inedible peels, stalks, and roots of veggies, and it can be used in many of the soup, bean, and gumbo recipes in this book.

TURNIP-THE-HEAT *butter bean* SOUP

• • • • • • •

serves **4 to 6**

I'm a hot girl who can almost always be spotted with hot-sauce-in-my-bag swag. Spicy food really has a certain magic to it. In the dead of winter, a hot and spicy dish will warm you to the core, and on a hot summer's night, it'll help you sweat to cool yourself in the heat. Southern folks love spicy food, and we also love butter beans and greens.

This chunky soup can be eaten with a chunk of Skillet Cornbread (page 102) to make it a complete and balanced meal.

½ pound dried butter beans or large lima beans, sorted, rinsed, and soaked for 8 hours

2 tablespoons coconut oil

1 large leek (white part only), thinly sliced

2 jalapeño peppers, seeded and minced (or keep a few seeds for spice)

Salt

6 cups Veggie Mineral Stock (page 88), 6 cups water plus 1 ½ vegetable bouillon cubes, or 6 cups water plus 2 teaspoons vegetable bouillon paste

1 (14-ounce) can diced tomatoes

1 bunch of turnip greens, stemmed and chopped

1 teaspoon freshly ground black pepper, plus more to taste

½ teaspoon cayenne pepper, plus more to taste

Hot sauce, for serving

1. Drain and rinse the soaked beans in a colander.

2. In a large heavy-bottomed pot, heat the oil over medium-high heat. Add the leek, jalapeños, and a pinch of salt and sauté until the leek begins to soften, about 3 minutes. Add the beans and stock and bring to a boil. Reduce the heat to medium-low and simmer for 45 minutes. The beans should be tender.

3. Reduce the heat to low and stir in the tomatoes, turnip greens, pepper, and cayenne. Continue to cook for 10 minutes, allowing the greens to wilt. Taste for seasoning and add more salt, pepper, and cayenne if desired. Serve with hot sauce on the side for more kick.

CURE-ALL
lentil
SOUP

• • • • • • • •

serves 4 to 6

In my household, we love soup! My guy likes to say that soup is his favorite food group. Of course, I also love it for how easy it is to prepare and how many nutrients I can pack into a single pot.

I call this soup the cure-all because of how rich and nutritious it is. For this recipe I channeled my nana's chicken noodle soup, which was loaded with carrots, celery, garlic, and onions. I replaced the chicken with lentils, which are a fantastic source of fiber, folate, and B vitamins as well as minerals like copper, zinc, and potassium. Zinc is known to support a healthy immune system and hormonal balance, and thanks to the antioxidant and antiviral power of garlic, this soup is sure to cure all.

2 tablespoons coconut oil

1 cup diced yellow onion

1 cup diced celery

3 garlic cloves, minced

1 cup diced carrots

1 unpeeled white potato, cut into ½-inch cubes

1 cup dried green lentils, sorted and rinsed

8 cups Veggie Mineral Stock (page 88), 8 cups water plus 2 vegetable bouillon cubes, or 8 teaspoons vegetable bouillon paste

1 teaspoon fennel seeds

1 teaspoon dried thyme

1 teaspoon celery seeds

½ teaspoon dried sage

1 bay leaf

1 tablespoon soy sauce

1 teaspoon white pepper

Salt

1. In a large heavy-bottomed pot, melt the oil over medium-high heat. Add the onion, celery, and garlic and sauté until the onion is translucent, about 3 minutes. Add the carrots, potato, lentils, and stock and bring to a boil. Reduce the heat to medium-low, then add the fennel seeds, thyme, celery seeds, sage, and bay leaf. Simmer for 30 minutes, or until the lentils become tender.

2. Season the soup with the soy sauce and white pepper. Season to taste with salt—you'll need to add more salt if you used the unsalted Veggie Mineral Stock, and less if you used the bouillon cubes or paste. Serve hot.

COCONUT CORN
CHOWDER, page 94

SWEET POTATO–
PARSNIP BISQUE,
page 95

coconut CORN CHOWDER

• • • • • • •

serves 4 to 6

This recipe has been a superstar on my blog since I created it in 2015. It's rich and creamy, tasty and nourishing, with juicy chunks of corn. It's unfortunate that corn gets such a bad reputation in the health food world. Corn, like other whole grains, is full of fiber and B-complex vitamins. Corn is also a great source of antioxidants, which help protect the body from free radical damage and premature aging. The starch in corn provides your brain and body with energy—all you've got to do is burn it!

For the tastiest and most nutritious chowder, use fresh corn when it's in season (but frozen corn will work when fresh isn't available). Enjoy this soup warm, at room temperature, or chilled.

2 tablespoons coconut oil

1 small red onion, diced

2 garlic cloves, minced

2 celery stalks, chopped (about 1½ cups)

2 medium carrots, chopped (about 1½ cups)

4 small Yukon Gold potatoes, peeled and cut into ½-inch cubes

2½ cups fresh corn kernels (from 4 ears) or frozen corn

1 (14-ounce) can full-fat coconut milk

2 cups Veggie Mineral Stock (page 88), or 2 cups water plus 2 teaspoons vegetable bouillon paste

1 teaspoon red chili flakes

1 teaspoon freshly ground black pepper, plus more to taste

Salt

1 cup chopped fresh cilantro, for garnish

1. In a large heavy-bottomed pot, melt the oil over medium-high heat. Add the onion, garlic, and celery and sauté until the onion is translucent, about 3 minutes. Stir in the carrots, potatoes, and corn. Pour in the coconut milk and add the stock. Bring to a boil, then reduce the heat to medium-low and simmer until the vegetables are tender, about 20 minutes.

2. Remove the pot from the heat. Once it has cooled for about 15 minutes, transfer about a third of the soup to a blender and puree until smooth. (Alternatively, blend the soup in the pot using a handheld immersion blender, being careful not to puree it completely.) Return the soup to the pot and add the red chili flakes and pepper.

3. Season to taste with salt and more pepper if necessary. Garnish with the cilantro and serve immediately or, if you prefer, at room temperature or chilled.

SWEET POTATO-PARSNIP bisque

• • • • • • •

serves 4

1 large or 2 small sweet potatoes, peeled and cut into ½-inch cubes (about 2 cups)

2 medium parsnips, peeled and chopped (about 1 ½ cups)

3 tablespoons grapeseed or coconut oil

2 garlic cloves, minced

1 teaspoon minced or grated peeled fresh ginger

2 cups cooked cannellini beans (see page 125) or 1 (15-ounce) can, drained and rinsed (reserve a handful for garnish)

2½ cups full-fat coconut milk

2 cups Veggie Mineral Stock (page 88), 2 cups water plus 1 teaspoon vegetable bouillon paste, or 2 cups water plus 1 vegetable bouillon cube

1 teaspoon freshly ground black pepper

½ teaspoon cayenne pepper

Chopped fresh parsley, for garnish

When I need comfort food, I sometimes eat cake or dark chocolate, but other times I crave a rich and creamy bisque. Instead of cream, this bisque relies on starchy sweet potatoes, tender white beans, and coconut milk to give it the most luxurious silky texture. In addition to its ability to replace dairy cream in most recipes, I love coconut milk for its nutritional profile. Though high in fat, coconuts contain fatty lauric acid, which may help lower LDL cholesterol, and medium-chain triglycerides (a type of fat), which your body and brain burn for energy. I recommend full-fat coconut milk because it will make the creamiest bisque and also because it is full of beneficial nutrients. Be sure to buy culinary coconut milk in a can or Tetra Pak carton, not coconut milk intended for drinking.

1. Preheat the oven to 375°F. Line a baking sheet with parchment paper and keep nearby.

2. In a large bowl, toss the sweet potatoes and parsnips with 1½ tablespoons of the oil. Arrange the vegetables evenly on the prepared baking sheet. Roast for 30 minutes, or until tender.

3. A few minutes before the vegetables are done, heat the remaining 1½ tablespoons oil in a large heavy-bottomed pot. Add the garlic and ginger and sauté until the garlic turns slightly golden. Be careful not to burn it.

4. Remove the roasted vegetables from the oven and add them to the pot along with the beans. Stir in the coconut milk and stock and bring to a boil. Reduce the heat to medium-low and simmer for 10 minutes to allow the flavors to incorporate. Remove from the heat and stir in the pepper and cayenne.

5. Using a handheld immersion blender, puree the soup until silky smooth. If you do not have one, let it cool, then transfer it to a blender for pureeing.

6. Garnish the bisque with parsley and the reserved beans and serve hot.

GREENS & SIDES

· ·

SOUL FOOD JUST AIN'T SOUL FOOD without cornbread, greens, and plenty of down-home sides. Folks might be impressed by the main attraction, but they really show up for the sides. Could you imagine Sunday dinner, Thanksgiving, or a summer cookout without sides? On the pages that follow, you'll find some of the South's most quintessential "side dishes" made without a lick of animal products. These vegan soul sides are just as delicious and alluring as the originals yet so much healthier. Tender Mess o' Collard Greens (page 103) are made succulent and smoky without the pork, Sweet Corn Succotash (page 109) is ultracomforting without butter, and "Sweet Jesus!" Mac & "Cheese" (page 113) gets a makeover without cholesterol-laden cheese.

   Like the salad and soup recipes, these side dishes can be mixed and matched to make a complete and balanced meal. Try the Skillet Cornbread (page 102) with the Pan-Fried Butter Beans & Greens (page 118) and Hickory Baked Beans (page 114). And what doesn't go well with Sensational Fried Green Tomatoes (page 107)?

   This chapter also features some perfect foods for entertaining with plenty of Southern hospitality: Dandelion Pesto Toasts (page 106), Crispy Battered Okra (page 119), Jalapeño Hush Puppies (page 104), Sweet Potato Hummus (page 121), and Black-eyed Pea Hummus (page 110). Your guests will feel so loved!

CREOLE
red bean
SAUSAGES

• • • • • • • •

makes 4 large sausages

There will be no pork on my fork. These vegan smoked kidney bean sausages will make you wonder why folks ever relied on animals for food. I ask myself that every time I use these in Bootylicious Gumbo (page 134), New Orleans–Style Red Beans & Rice (page 140), Low Country Grits (page 60), or Tender Mess o' Collard Greens (page 103).

These satisfying sausages are made using wheat gluten (aka seitan, aka wheat meat, aka kalebone). This ultrameaty ingredient has its roots in sixth-century China, where it was used—and still is—to replace meat, especially by vegetarian Buddhists. Though it's plagued by a myth that it is highly processed, wheat gluten is simply the gluten that is left over after hydrating and separating starch from wheat flour. It's so simple you can do it at home. Make sure your kidney beans are well cooked and soft. Hard beans aren't good for you, and they won't work well in this recipe either.

1 cup cooked kidney beans (see page 125) or a little less than half a 15-ounce can

¼ cup Veggie Mineral Stock (page 88) or ¼ cup water plus ¼ vegetable bouillon cube

1 tablespoon pure maple syrup

1 tablespoon olive oil

1 ½ tablespoons soy sauce

1 tablespoon white or yellow miso

1 garlic clove, minced

¼ cup minced Vidalia onion

2 teaspoons smoked paprika

1 teaspoon dried thyme

1 teaspoon fennel seeds

2 teaspoons Creole Seasoning (page 36)

¾ cup vital wheat gluten

1 tablespoon potato starch

1. Place the beans in a large bowl and mash with a fork until they are mostly creamy; the texture should be a bit chunky. Add the remaining ingredients and stir well to thoroughly combine. You may need to use your hands, as the batter will be very thick. Form the batter into a ball.

2. Divide the ball into 4 sections and use your hands to form each section into a sausage shape. Make sure to pack the batter tightly as you shape it. Wrap each sausage tightly in about a square-foot sheet of aluminum foil, twisting the ends to seal the sausage inside.

3. Set a steaming basket over 1 to 2 inches of boiling water, add the sausages, tightly cover, and steam for 45 minutes. Keep an eye on the water level and replenish when necessary.

4. Remove the sausages from the heat and let cool until safe to handle. Place the sausages, still wrapped in foil, in the refrigerator to firm for at least 3 hours or up to overnight. (You could eat them right away, but the texture isn't ideal yet.) They will keep fresh for up to 7 days in the refrigerator.

5. When ready to use, slice the sausages and pan-fry them to reheat before serving or add directly into other recipes that call for vegan sausage.

SKILLET
CORNBREAD,
page 102

RED PEPPER
AIOLI, page 209

JALAPEÑO HUSH
PUPPIES, page 104

TENDER MESS O'
COLLARD GREENS,
page 103

skillet CORNBREAD

· · · · · · · ·

serves 9

If I know one thing for sure, it's that every cook has their own style and preference for cornbread. Some like it cakey and sweet; some like it savory. I like a crumbly cornbread and use mostly cornmeal, but if you prefer a cakier texture, half cornmeal and half flour is the way to go. Some cooks add jalapeño peppers, green onions, or canned corn, but the rest of us like to keep it simple. Depending on the state, town, family name, and grandmama recipe, Southern cooks do it differently, and I think that's just fine.

I love this simple and moist recipe for corn-forward skillet pone. If you like a little color and heat, feel free to mix in ¼ cup of scallions, a seeded and minced jalapeño, 1 cup frozen or fresh corn (from 1 ear of corn), 1 cup vegan creamed corn (use ½ cup less soy milk), and/or 1 cup of vegan cheddar "cheese."

2 tablespoons ground flaxseed meal

1¾ cups yellow or white cornmeal

½ cup spelt flour or whole wheat pastry flour

1½ teaspoons baking powder

½ teaspoon baking soda

2 teaspoons salt

2 tablespoons cane sugar

1½ cups plain unsweetened soy milk or other nondairy milk

2 teaspoons apple cider vinegar or white vinegar

¼ cup canola or grapeseed oil

1. Preheat the oven to 350°F. Grease a 12-inch cast-iron skillet and set nearby.

2. In a medium bowl, stir together the flaxseed meal and 6 tablespoons water. Set it aside to thicken for at least 3 minutes.

3. Meanwhile, in large medium bowl, whisk together the cornmeal, flour, baking powder, baking soda, salt, and sugar.

4. Add the soy milk, vinegar, and oil to the bowl with the flaxseed meal mixture and whisk well until creamy. Pour the wet ingredients into the dry ingredients and gently stir until just combined. Do not overmix.

5. Pour the batter into the prepared skillet and bake for 20 minutes, or until a toothpick comes out clean.

6. Let the cornbread cool in the skillet for at least 10 minutes before serving. The cornbread will keep for up to 3 days in an airtight container at room temperature.

TENDER *mess o'* COLLARD GREENS

•••••••

serves **4**

Every January 1 my family and I eat collard greens with tender Good Luck Black-eyed Peas (page 153) and Skillet Cornbread (page 102) to celebrate the new year. In Southern lore this New Year's Day staple will bring money (collards) and lots of luck (black-eyed peas). I'm not usually superstitious, but this is one tradition I won't skip.

Collard greens definitely shouldn't be relegated to one special day, though. This dark leafy green is a rich source of vitamin K, vitamin A, insoluble fiber, calcium, and so much more. There are countless ways to cook collards. I like collards cooked with acidic tomatoes to help balance their bitterness. The smoked paprika and soy sauce are the winning combination to elevate collards to a signature comfort food. For extra smokiness, serve the finished collards with a few slices of lightly pan-fried Creole Red Bean Sausages (page 99).

2 tablespoons grapeseed or canola oil

3 garlic cloves, minced

2 large ripe tomatoes, diced, or 1 (14-ounce) can of diced tomatoes

2 large bunches of collard greens, tough stems removed and leaves thinly sliced into ¼-inch ribbons (see Note)

Sea salt

3 tablespoons soy sauce, plus more to taste

1 tablespoon smoked paprika

1. In a large heavy-bottomed pot, heat the oil over medium heat. Add the garlic, reduce the heat to medium-low, and sauté until it begins to turn golden. Be careful not to burn it.

2. Stir in the tomatoes and cook until soft, about 3 minutes—or 2 minutes for canned tomatoes. Add the collard ribbons and a sprinkle of salt and stir well. Reduce the heat to low and cover the greens. Cook until tender, about 30 minutes or longer, depending on your preference.

3. Remove from the heat and stir in the soy sauce and paprika. Taste for seasoning and add more soy sauce if desired.

NOTE: The way greens are cut plays a role in how they taste and how tender they get when cooked. Different cooks cut their greens differently, but my nana taught me to cut collards and other greens (including herbs like basil) into thin ribbons. After thoroughly washing your collard leaves in a large basin, use a paring knife to remove the tough stem in the center. Stack 5 to 10 leaves on top of each other, then tightly roll them into a log shape. Use a sharp knife to thinly slice the rolled leaves into thin ribbons about ¼ inch thick. The technical term for this method is *chiffonade*, though we never called it that. Cutting greens this way will help them cook more quickly and become wonderfully tender. This same method can be used for any type of dark leafy green or large leaf herbs like basil.

JALAPEÑO HUSH PUPPIES

• • • • • • •

serves **4** to **6**

1 cup plain unsweetened soy milk or other nondairy milk, at room temperature

1 teaspoon white vinegar

2 tablespoons ground flaxseed meal

1 cup cornmeal

1 cup unbleached all-purpose flour

½ teaspoon baking soda

1 teaspoon salt

2 tablespoons grapeseed, canola, or safflower oil, plus 1 quart for frying

4 green onions, minced

1 jalapeño pepper, seeded and minced

I've never met a single person who doesn't love hush puppies: tender and airy deep-fried cornmeal balls. In my research for this book, I discovered that these simple dough drops have a not-so-simple history. They apparently were made famous in the late 1800s by Romeo Govan, a much-respected black chef who hosted and fed fishermen at his "clubhouse" along South Carolina's Edisto River. Govan called them red horse bread, probably because they were served alongside a fish called red horse that he'd fry up. *Hush puppy* first appeared in print as a reference to gravy but in the 1900s morphed to refer to the delicious fried cornmeal we all love today.

Serve your hush puppies along with the Peach-Date BBQ Jackfruit Sliders (page 135), Rainbow Root Slaw (page 79), or on their own.

1. In a small bowl, stir together the soy milk and vinegar to make a vegan buttermilk. Set it aside to thicken and curdle for 5 minutes.

2. In another small bowl, stir together the flaxseed meal and ¼ cup of water. Set it aside to thicken for at least 3 minutes.

3. In a medium bowl, whisk together the cornmeal, flour, baking soda, and salt.

4. Pour the buttermilk mixture into the flaxseed meal mixture. Add the 2 tablespoons oil and whisk to combine. Pour the wet mixture into the dry and stir well. Fold in the green onions and jalapeño.

5. In a large dutch oven, heat the quart of oil to 350°F. Double-line a large plate with paper towels and keep nearby.

6. Use a cookie scooper to scoop balls of batter—each one should be about 2 tablespoons' worth—directly into the hot oil. Add as many scoops as you can fit in at a time without overcrowding. Gently stir them with a wooden spoon. Once they float to the surface and turn a golden color, they are done. Use a slotted spoon to transfer them to the prepared plate. Repeat with the remaining batter.

7. Serve with Cinnamon-Honee Butter (page 45, but hold the cinnamon) or as they are.

DANDELION *pesto* TOASTS

• • • • • • •

makes 1½ cups pesto

When spring rolls around make sure to stock your refrigerator with dandelion greens. This bitter green is great for cleansing the liver, plus it's high in lots of crucial nutrients: calcium, lutein, vitamin A, and iron. This pesto is my favorite way to enjoy dandelion greens. The pumpkin seeds are a great source of zinc, magnesium, iron, and vitamin E. I like to serve this pesto on sourdough toasts, but I also think it's delicious on crackers, added to sandwiches, and tossed with pasta.

3 cups dandelion greens

2 large garlic cloves

¾ cup toasted pumpkin seeds (see Note on page 164)

Juice from ½ lime

1 teaspoon sea salt

½ teaspoon chili powder

¼ cup olive oil, plus more for drizzling

2 slices of crusty sourdough bread

Red chili flakes, for garnish

1. Place the dandelion greens, garlic, pumpkin seeds, lime juice, salt, and chili powder in a food processor and blend until combined. Slowly pour in the oil while the food processor is still running and continue to blend another 30 seconds, or until your desired texture is reached. If you prefer a thinner pesto, blend in 2 tablespoons water or oil.

2. Toast the bread on both sides until golden around the edges. Top the toast with pesto and drizzle a teaspoon or so of oil over the top. Garnish with a dash of red chili flakes and serve immediately. Store the pesto in an airtight container in the refrigerator for up to 3 days. The dandelion will darken in color, but it is still okay to eat.

SENSATIONAL FRIED GREEN tomatoes

· · · · · · ·

serves 4

There are few things as delicious as fried green tomatoes: crispy on the outside, juicy and warm on the inside, and full of flavor all around.

Green tomatoes are simply unripe tomatoes, not an exotic variety. However, outside of the South, green tomatoes are elusive. I buy them at my local farmers' markets in the summertime when tomatoes are at their peak. I will happily eat a plate of these on their own, but they make a lovely addition to Purple and White Potato Salad (page 82) and Bourbon BBQ Tempeh Sandwiches (page 142).

NOTE: To test the heat of frying oil, stick a wooden spoon into the oil, and if tiny bubbles form around the spoon, it is hot enough to use.

2 tablespoons ground flaxseed meal

½ cup soymilk

1 cup unbleached all-purpose flour

1 cup rice flour

½ cup cornmeal

½ cup panko bread crumbs

2 teaspoons coarse kosher salt

¼ teaspoon freshly ground black pepper

1 quart vegetable oil, for frying

4 large green tomatoes, sliced ½ inch thick

1. In a small bowl, stir together the flaxseed meal and ¼ cup water. Let it thicken for at least 3 minutes, then whisk in the soy milk.

2. In a medium bowl, combine the flours, cornmeal, panko, salt, and pepper.

3. In a large cast-iron skillet or dutch oven, heat the oil to 350°F. If you don't have a thermometer, test the temperature using the wooden spoon trick (see Note). Double-line a large plate with paper towels and keep nearby.

4. Use 1 hand to dip each slice of tomato into the wet mixture, then drop it into the flour mixture. Use your dry hand to coat it completely. Carefully drop the coated tomatoes into the oil and fry on each side for about 3 minutes, or until the batter becomes golden brown. Be careful not to overcrowd the pan when frying the tomatoes.

5. Transfer the fried tomatoes to the prepared plate and serve hot.

SWEET CORN *succotash*

● ● ● ● ● ● ●

serves 4

I grew up thinking of succotash as a quintessential soul food staple, but it turns out that this dish of sweet corn and lima beans was introduced to English colonizers by the Wampanoag tribe in what is now known as New England. The Narragansett name of this dish was *msíckquatash*, and like today's version, it consisted of boiled sweet corn (either dried or fresh, depending on the time of year) and beans.

One of my nana's most requested dishes is her succotash. I veganized her famous version and added some jalapeño pepper because I love the spice! But you can leave out the jalapeño if you have a lower tolerance for heat—this succotash is delicious either way.

2 tablespoons coconut or grapeseed oil

1 cup chopped Vidalia onion

2 garlic cloves, minced

½ jalapeño pepper, seeded and minced

1 pound frozen or fresh green baby lima beans

1 cup fresh corn kernels (from 1 ear) or frozen

½ cup plain unsweetened soy milk or full-fat coconut milk

1 ½ teaspoons salt, plus more to taste

1 teaspoon freshly ground black pepper, plus more to taste

1. In a heavy-bottomed pot, heat the oil over medium-high heat. Add the onion, garlic, and jalapeño and sauté, stirring occasionally, until the onion is translucent, about 3 minutes.

2. Add the beans, corn, soy milk, and salt. Reduce the heat to medium-low. Stir well, cover, and simmer for 30 minutes, stirring occasionally.

3. Season to taste with more salt and the pepper. Serve warm or at room temperature.

BLACK-EYED PEA
hummus

• • • • • • • •

makes 1½ cups

For years I wouldn't eat black-eyed peas in any way other than stewed with garlic, onions, celery, and traditional spices. Every other preparation seemed to mask the unique flavor of my favorite bean, and I just couldn't stand to lose that. This creamy black-eyed pea hummus does a great job of maintaining all the magic of this little legume while using it in a fresh and delicious way. I love eating this hummus with raw veggies, on crackers, or sandwiched between bread with roasted veggies.

1 garlic clove

1½ cups cooked black-eyed peas (see page 125) or 1 (15-ounce) can, drained and rinsed

¼ cup tahini

2 tablespoons olive oil

1 tablespoon freshly squeezed lemon juice

1 teaspoon ground cumin

½ teaspoon smoked paprika

½ teaspoon salt

Dash of cayenne pepper

1. Place the garlic in your food processor, and blend until it is minced. Add the black-eyed peas, tahini, oil, lemon juice, cumin, paprika, salt, and cayenne and blend until smooth. If needed, add 2 to 4 tablespoons of water to thin the hummus.

2. Serve the hummus with raw vegetables, chips, or bread. It can also be added to sandwiches and salads. It will keep fresh in the refrigerator for up to 7 days.

CANDIED
yams

• • • • • • • •

serves **4** to **6**

4 **large sweet potatoes**
2 **tablespoons granulated sugar**
2 **tablespoons brown sugar**
½ **teaspoon ground cinnamon**
½ **teaspoon freshly grated nutmeg**
Pinch of ground cloves
1 **tablespoon vegan butter, at room temperature**
2 **tablespoons coconut oil**

I hadn't had candied yams in many, many years when I cooked these up. Steeped in culture shock in Boston, I yearned more than ever for my nana's home cooking and soul food. I've talked a lot of how much I've always loved sweet potato pie, but I love candied yams just as much. These make use of coconut oil, which is one of the best ingredients to pair with sweet potatoes!

1. Place the sweet potatoes in a large pot, cover with water, and bring to a boil. Cook until tender, about 20 minutes.

2. Drain the potatoes in a colander. When they are cool enough to handle but still warm, peel them with your hands.

3. Preheat the oven to 350°F.

4. In a small bowl, mix together both sugars, the cinnamon, nutmeg, and cloves.

5. Quarter the sweet potatoes and place half of them into an 8 × 8-inch baking dish. Place ½ tablespoon of the vegan butter in small clumps on the sweet potatoes and drizzle with 1 tablespoon of the coconut oil. Evenly sprinkle half of the sugar mixture over the top. Layer the remaining potato quarters over the first layer and add the remaining ½ tablespoon vegan butter, 1 tablespoon coconut oil, and the sugar mixture. Bake for 40 minutes, until the potatoes are very tender.

6. Remove from the oven and let the candied yams cool for at least 10 minutes before serving.

"sweet jesus!"
MAC &
"CHEESE"

· · · · · · ·

serves **4**

Who do we have to thank for macaroni and cheese? None other than one of America's founding fathers, Thomas Jefferson, and his slave chef James Hemings. Jefferson loved food, especially fancy European fare, and brought Hemings along with him while living in France as George Washington's minister of trade. While in France, Hemings studied with the premier chefs at Château de Chantilly and picked up one very special dish that would become a staple of Southern cooking, macaroni and cheese made with loads of butter and cheese. I doubt they would have had any idea that we'd one day be making rich and cheesy mac and "cheese" without animal products.

This recipe is a riff on the version by Angela Liddon of *Oh She Glows*. I swapped out butternut squash for sweet potato, added roasted garlic to give it more depth, used plenty of nutritional yeast, and topped it off with Crispy Eggplant Bacon (page 55) for Southern charm.

2 garlic cloves

1 teaspoon grapeseed oil

¾ cup plain unsweetened soy milk or other nondairy milk

1½ tablespoons arrowroot powder or cornstarch

4 tablespoons vegan butter or grapeseed oil

1 cup nutritional yeast, plus more to taste

3 teaspoons Dijon mustard

1 teaspoon onion powder

1½ teaspoons sea salt, plus more to taste

½ tablespoon freshly squeezed lemon juice or apple cider vinegar

½ pound elbow pasta or your favorite macaroni noodles

2 cups mashed sweet potato (from 2 baked medium sweet potatoes)

½ recipe Crispy Eggplant Bacon (page 55), optional

1. Preheat the oven to 375°F. Place the garlic cloves on a small sheet of aluminum foil, and drizzle the grapeseed oil on top. Fold the sides of the foil over the garlic and place it on a baking sheet. Roast for 30 minutes until soft. You can do this while you're working on the other ingredients.

2. In a small bowl, combine ¼ cup of the soy milk with the arrowroot powder. Stir well to dissolve any clumps and set aside.

3. In a medium saucepan, heat the vegan butter over medium heat. Whisk in the remaining ½ cup soy milk, the nutritional yeast, mustard, onion powder, salt, and lemon juice. Add the soy milk–arrowroot powder mixture, stirring well as it thickens. Once thick, remove the pan from the heat.

4. In a large pot, cook the pasta according to the package instructions. Drain it in a colander and place in a deep baking dish to cool.

5. Transfer the sauce to a blender and add the mashed sweet potato and roasted garlic. Puree until super smooth and season to taste with more nutritional yeast and salt. It should be pretty salty to balance the pasta.

6. Pour the "cheese" sauce over the pasta and stir well. Cover with aluminum foil and bake for 20 minutes, or until warmed. Top with eggplant bacon and serve immediately.

hickory
BAKED
BEANS

• • • • • • •

serves 6

My family always used canned Bush's vegetarian baked beans, and my nana would often make them for me with chunks of turkey hot dogs—aptly named hot dogs and baked beans. It was one of my top five favorite meals as a kid.

As an adult and chef, I prefer to prepare classics from scratch to avoid excess sugar, salt, and harmful canning chemicals like BPA. I was surprised to discover how easy baked beans are to make at home. Not as easy as opening a can and heating the contents, but much more satisfying and delicious.

For this recipe I use hickory syrup, a delightful syrup made with roasted hickory bark foraged from Virginia forests. It gives these baked beans a distinctive flavor, but if you don't have any, you can use maple syrup.

1 pound dried navy beans, sorted, rinsed, and soaked for 8 hours

1 bay leaf

1 tablespoon arrowroot powder

2 tablespoons grapeseed oil

¼ cup diced yellow onion

3 garlic cloves, minced

1 vegetable bouillon cube or 2 teaspoons vegetable bouillon paste

¼ cup sugar-sweetened ketchup

¼ cup hickory syrup or pure maple syrup

2 tablespoons tamari soy sauce, plus more to taste

2 tablespoons apple cider vinegar

2 tablespoons Dijon mustard

2 tablespoons brown sugar

1 tablespoon vegan Worcestershire sauce

3 teaspoons smoked paprika

2 teaspoons liquid smoke

1. Drain and rinse the soaked beans in a colander.

2. In a large heavy-bottomed pot, bring 6 cups water to a boil and add the beans. Reduce the heat to medium-low and add the bay leaf. Partially cover the pot with a lid and let simmer for 45 to 60 minutes, or until the beans are tender. Reserve 1 cup of the cooking liquid, drain the beans in a colander, and set both aside.

3. Preheat the oven to 375°F.

4. Add the arrowroot powder to the reserved cup of the bean liquid and stir well to remove any clumps. In the same pot you cooked the beans in, heat the oil on medium heat and add the onion and garlic. Sauté until the onion is translucent, about 3 minutes. Add the bean liquid mixture, the bouillon cube, ketchup, hickory syrup, tamari, vinegar, mustard, brown sugar, vegan Worcestershire sauce, paprika, and liquid smoke to the beans. Stir well, taste for seasoning, and add more tamari if desired. Cover the pot with a lid, place it in the oven, and bake for 30 minutes, or until the top looks slightly dry and the liquid has reduced. Serve hot.

CARIBBEAN *steamed* CABBAGE

· · · · · · · ·

serves 4

2 tablespoons grapeseed or coconut oil

1 medium onion, thinly sliced

1 garlic clove, minced

1 jalapeño pepper, minced (seeds removed if you want it less spicy)

1 small head of green cabbage, outer leaves and core removed, thinly sliced

1 cup diced carrots

1 teaspoon dried thyme

¼ teaspoon allspice

1 teaspoon salt, plus more to taste

1 teaspoon freshly ground black pepper

This recipe is inspired by the spicy Jamaican cabbage I love so much. During slavery, the majority of African slaves were taken to the Caribbean and South America. Caribbean slaves were often sold to North American masters, leading to an early exchange of culture among Africans, native peoples, and Europeans. Cabbage came from Europe but over centuries has become a staple food in the diets of Caribbean and North American blacks. Allspice, an essential spice in Caribbean culture, is from a tree native to the Caribbean, Central America, and southern Mexico. The combination of ingredients from different regions is part of what makes the history of black soul food so interesting and the food delicious.

In a large heavy-bottomed pot, heat the oil over medium heat and add the onion, garlic, and jalapeño. Sauté until the onion is translucent, about 3 minutes. Reduce the heat to medium-low and add the cabbage, carrots, thyme, allspice, and salt. Stir well and cook until the cabbage is tender, about 20 minutes, stirring occasionally. If the cabbage starts to dry out, add 2 to 4 tablespoons water. Be careful not to burn it. Stir in the pepper, taste for seasoning, and add more salt if desired.

SPICY FRIED CAULIFLOWER
"CHICKEN," page 152

PAN-FRIED BUTTER
BEANS & GREENS,
page 118

SWEET POTATO
HUMMUS, page 121

PAN-FRIED BUTTER BEANS & greens

• • • • • • •

serves **2 to 4**

I consider starchy butter beans to be one of the most satisfying foods. Pan-fried, their skins form a crispy coating, which pairs perfectly with the bitterness of tender mustard greens. This dish is perfect for any night of the week, or it can be whipped up quickly to serve in a more formal setting, say Thanksgiving or Christmas dinner. Look for very fresh mustard greens, and if possible, prepare you own butter beans (aka large lima beans). If you cannot find mustards, you can use collards or kale.

2 tablespoons grapeseed oil

2 garlic cloves, minced

1 ½ cups cooked butter beans or large lima beans (see page 125) or 1 (15-ounce) can, drained and rinsed

1 bunch of mustard greens, chopped

¼ cup Veggie Mineral Stock (page 88) or water

Salt to taste

Freshly ground black pepper to taste

1. Line a large plate with paper towels and set aside. In a large skillet, heat the oil over medium heat. Add the garlic and sauté until it begins to turn golden, about 30 seconds. Be careful not to burn it. Stir in the beans and pan-fry until they begin to char and brown, about 5 minutes.

2. Using a slotted spoon, remove the beans to the prepared plate, leaving behind as much of the garlic as possible.

3. Add the mustard greens and stock to the skillet and stir. Cook until the greens are tender, about 10 minutes.

4. Season to taste with salt and pepper—start with ¼ teaspoon of each. Serve the greens topped with the pan-fried butter beans.

CRISPY *battered* OKRA

• • • • • • • •

serves 4

Fried okra is finger-lickin' good and so easy to make. This is a great recipe to get kids and picky folks to eat nutritious, fiber-rich okra. Presoaking the okra in cold water with lemon or lime juice will get rid of some of its natural sliminess.

1 pound okra, cut into ¼-inch slices

Juice of 1 lemon or lime

½ cup plain unsweetened soy milk or other nondairy milk

½ cup unbleached all-purpose flour

½ cup cornmeal

½ teaspoon salt

½ teaspoon freshly ground black pepper

1 teaspoon Creole Seasoning (page 36)

1 cup coconut or grapeseed oil

1. Place the sliced okra in a medium bowl, add the lemon juice, and cover with water. Soak for 15 to 20 minutes. Rinse well after soaking, pat the okra dry, and set aside.

2. Pour the soy milk into a medium bowl and set aside.

3. In a large bowl, stir together the flour, cornmeal, salt, pepper, and Creole seasoning.

4. In a large heavy-bottomed pot or cast-iron skillet, heat the oil to 350°F. Double-line a large plate with paper towels and set aside.

5. Add the okra to the soy milk and stir. Drain the okra in a colander, then place it into the cornmeal mixture. Toss the okra around in the bowl until each piece is coated.

6. Use a dry hand to carefully remove each piece of okra and add it to the hot oil. Fry on each side for 3 to 4 minutes, until golden.

7. Transfer the fried okra to the prepared plate and serve hot.

SWEET POTATO *hummus*

• • • • • • •

makes 2½ cups

Hummus is not Southern, but sweet potatoes sure are. Add some love and you've got a modern soul food creation. This recipe marries one of my favorite dips with my favorite vegetable, and the result is nothing short of absolutely delicious. This recipe calls for miso, an unlikely and un-Southern ingredient that adds a certain richness to the hummus. For the best results, use a home-baked sweet potato, not canned.

1 garlic clove, chopped

1½ cups cooked chickpeas (see page 125) or 1 (15-ounce) can, drained and rinsed

1 cup mashed sweet potato (from 1 baked medium sweet potato)

1 tablespoon fennel seeds

1 teaspoon ground cumin

2 teaspoons white or yellow miso

3 tablespoons tahini

1 teaspoon freshly squeezed lemon juice

1 teaspoon balsamic vinegar

½ teaspoon cayenne pepper

1 teaspoon freshly ground black pepper

Salt to taste

1. Place the garlic in your food processor, and blend until it is minced. Add the remaining ingredients and blend until very smooth and creamy. Adjust any of the seasonings, and add salt to taste.

2. Serve the hummus with raw vegetables, chips, or bread. It can also be added to sandwiches and salads. It will keep fresh in the refrigerator for up to 7 days.

MAINS

• •

WELCOME TO THE MAIN ATTRACTION! There's a notion that vegan food is just side dishes and salads, but that just isn't so (though we do love our sides and salads). On the pages that follow you'll find entrées special enough for Christmas dinner, like Cornbread Dressing (page 132), and practical enough for an easy weeknight meal, such as Happy Hearts "Crab" Cakes (page 129) and Sweet Potato Burgers (page 156). If you're looking for a something meaty, try the Peach-Date BBQ Jackfruit Sliders (page 135) or the Spicy Fried Cauliflower "Chicken" (page 152).

For these delicious main dishes, we're using wholesome and nutritious plants to replace animal products. Foods like green jackfruit, cauliflower, oyster mushrooms, and tempeh will make you forget all about the meat. Texture-wise, these whole foods make great meat replacements, but they also happen to be much more nutritious than animal meat and even processed vegan meats.

One of my most important tips to maintain a healthy lifestyle is to be prepared. That means keeping your refrigerator, cabinets, and pantry stocked with wholesome ingredients so that you can easily throw together a meal. That also means meal prep. Spending a couple of hours a week to prepare meals for the coming days is one of the best ways to eat well. You should set yourself up to come home from work, open the fridge, and find an exciting assortment of meals (or at the very least, one exciting meal). The recipes in this chapter are perfect to get you excited about healthy eating because they're comforting and bursting with flavor. I recommend getting started with the Jackfruit Jambalaya (page 137), New Orleans–Style Red Beans & Rice (page 140), Southern Buddha Bowl (page 131), and Smoky Black-eyed Pea Cakes (page 154), though everything is really darn good.

perfect
POT O' BEANS

· · · · · · ·

serves 6 to 8

This recipe will work with any beans, and the cooked beans may be used for any recipe calling for beans in this cookbook. I make at least one pot of beans each week to add to soups, salads, Buddha bowls, or burgers. Preparing your own beans at home is a great way to save money and optimize nutrition.

1 pound dried beans, such as black beans but any kind will do, sorted, rinsed, and soaked for 8 hours

5 to 6 cups Veggie Mineral Stock (page 88) or water

1 bay leaf

1 medium chopped yellow onion (optional)

2 garlic cloves, minced

1 cup chopped celery

2 teaspoons salt

2 tablespoons grapeseed oil or other type of oil (optional)

1. Drain and rinse the soaked beans in a colander, then transfer them to a dutch oven and cover with the stock. Cover the pot with a lid and bring to a boil. Skim off any white foam that floats on top.

2. Reduce the heat to medium-low and add the bay leaf, onion, garlic, and celery. Simmer until the beans are tender, about 60 minutes for most beans, but up to 90 minutes for black beans and red beans. Check the doneness of your beans at the 45- and 60-minute mark.

3. Season with salt in the last 5 minutes of cooking. If you'd like creamier beans, add a couple tablespoons of oil, or use a spoon to mash some of the beans on the side of the pot.

BEAN-COOKING CHART

BEAN	SOAK TIME	COOK TIME
RED BEANS/KIDNEY BEANS	8 hours	60–90 minutes
BLACK-EYED PEAS	Not necessary, but I soak them for 8 hours anyway	60–90 minutes
BUTTER BEANS/LARGE LIMA BEANS	8 hours	45–60 minutes
BABY LIMA BEANS	8 hours	60 minutes
LENTILS (green, black, brown)	Not necessary	30–45 minutes
CANNELLINI BEANS	8 hours	60–90 minutes
NAVY BEANS	8 hours	60–90 minutes
PINTO BEANS	8 hours	60–90 minutes
BLACK BEANS	8 hours	60–90 minutes
CHICKPEAS/GARBANZO BEANS	8 hours	60–90 minutes

Note that older dried beans may take longer to cook.

HOW TO COOK BEANS

Knowing how to make a perfect pot of beans is one of the essential tools of Southern cooking. We love our beans down South and use them in an incredible variety of ways: black-eyed pea cakes, red beans and rice, dips and hummus, and creamy soups. Though the recipes in this book don't require home-cooked beans, I highly recommend them. Cooking your own beans at home is (1) easy, (2) much less expensive than canned, (3) more nutritious (none of that BPA and salt), and (4) the tastiest way! You can also control the texture of your beans better when making them at home. There's nothing worse than opening a can of overly firm beans.

Though cooking beans is supereasy, most legumes need to be soaked. To avoid having to do this multiple times per week, I like to cook a couple of pots o' beans and store them in my freezer for use later. That way, enjoying delicious and nutritious home-cooked beans is just as easy as opening a can.

If you are especially sensitive to the indigestible sugars in beans, try reducing their gassy effect by cooking them with a sheet of kombu seaweed. But remember, the secret to being able to digest beans without any issues is to eat them more often. As your body becomes accustomed to their fiber and starches, any discomfort or flatulence will subside.

KEYS TO TENDER CREAMY BEANS

1. Quality of beans: Make sure your beans are of high quality and fresh. Even dried beans can get stale. Dried beans that are kept beyond their expiration date should be relegated to being pie weights; cooking them would only be a letdown. My favorite beans come from Camellia Brand in New Orleans. For fancy heirloom beans, I buy from Rancho Gordo in California.

2. Cook time: Beans must be simmered until they are tender, which, depending on the bean, may take anywhere from 30 to 90 minutes. I cook all my beans for at least 45 minutes, then poke and taste them to test doneness. Undercooked beans are a pain to digest and no fun to eat, so be patient with your legumes.

3. Cooking method: Avoid acidic ingredients when cooking beans. Add things like tomatoes, vinegar, or citrus near the end of cooking, once the beans are already tender. Cooking beans at a rolling boil will cause them to lose their shape and become mushy. Cook beans at a gentle simmer and add salt.

4. Fat: Cooking beans with fat helps to make them creamy and absorb the flavor of your seasonings. Down south the tradition is to cook beans with fatty chunks of meat and/or sausage, lard, or butter. Luckily you can enjoy the fatty goodness without animal products. Sauté your aromatics (onion, garlic, celery) in a couple of healthy glugs of canola, grapeseed, olive, or coconut oil. You may also add a few tablespoons of your favorite oil during the last 10 or so minutes of cooking to give them a creamier feel.

5. Mash them: Bean stews like Good Luck Black-eyed Peas (page 153) or New Orleans–Style Red Beans & Rice (page 140) require some mashing. Once they're tender, take your wooden spoon and mash some of the beans on the side of the pot until your desired texture is reached. You may also add a few tablespoons of your favorite oil in the last 10 or so minutes of cooking to give them a creamier feel.

HAPPY HEARTS "crab" CAKES

• • • • • • •

makes about 12 cakes

My dad's family lives in Maryland, land of the blue crab and Old Bay seasoning. I was a picky eater as a kid, but I had no problem opening a boiled crab to get to the meat. Crab cakes, on the other hand, weren't as easy to like—too much mayonnaise! Like so many Southern dishes I disliked as a kid, I fell in love with the vegan version. These fabulous and compassionate "crab" cakes channel the flavors and textures of those popular Maryland cakes, only without the pound of mayo. To replicate the texture of crabmeat, I use hearts of palm—a common vegan substitute for crabmeat—and chickpeas for body. Old Bay seasoning is the key to legitimizing these cakes, while *ume* plum vinegar lends an extra seafood kick. These "crab" cakes got me my first *Today* show appearance in 2016 and have blown away many people!

2 (14-ounce) cans hearts of palm, drained and chopped into large pieces

1½ cups cooked chickpeas (see page 125) or 1 (15-ounce) can, drained and rinsed

1 cup panko bread crumbs, plus ½ cup for coating

¼ cup vegan mayonnaise

1 jalapeño pepper, seeded and minced

1½ tablespoons Old Bay seasoning

1 teaspoon *ume* plum vinegar

1 teaspoon Dijon mustard

6 tablespoons grapeseed, canola, or safflower oil

1. Place the hearts of palm and chickpeas in a food processor and pulse to combine and mash. Don't overprocess it; you still want some "crabby" texture.

2. Scrape the hearts of palm mixture into a large bowl and add the 1 cup panko, vegan mayonnaise, jalapeño, Old Bay seasoning, vinegar, and mustard. Stir well to combine.

3. Line a large plate with paper towels and keep nearby.

4. In a large skillet, heat the oil over medium-high heat. Place the ½ cup panko in a shallow dish. Form the "crab" mixture into 2-inch-wide patties, making sure to pack the mixture tightly, and then coat them in the panko in the shallow dish. Place the patties in the skillet (do not overcrowd) and pan-fry for 3 minutes on each side. Transfer the patties to the prepared plate. Repeat with the remaining mixture.

5. Serve with a dollop of Red Pepper Aioli (page 209) and fresh greens.

MAPLE SAUSAGE *ciabatta* FILLING

• • • • • • • •

serves **4 to 6**

Before I became vegan, my nana's turkey filling was on my list of top-five favorite foods. We would eat it every Thanksgiving and sometimes on Christmas, too. Beyond the delicious taste and satisfying texture, I could feel my nana's love in every bite. Though I stopped eating turkey in 2008, it took me until 2013 to create a vegan version of Nana's excellent stuffing. I'm proud to say that Nana approves, and so do I. One note for when you're preparing this: the most important ingredient is l-o-v-e.

This stuffing can be made 3 days in advance—just hold off on adding the stock until you're ready to bake.

1 loaf of ciabatta bread, cut into ⅓-inch cubes (6 to 8 cups)

5 tablespoons grapeseed oil

1 (1-pound) butternut squash, cut into ⅓-inch cubes (about 2 cups)

1 medium yellow onion, diced

4 garlic cloves, minced

1 cup diced celery

Sea salt

10 ounces fresh shiitake mushrooms, stems removed, tops sliced (about 2 cups)

2 Smoky White Bean Sausages (page 59), diced

6 fresh sage leaves, minced

1 tablespoon minced fresh rosemary

1 teaspoon white pepper

2 cups Veggie Mineral Stock (page 88), 2 cups water plus 2 teaspoons vegetable bouillon paste, or 2 cups water plus 1 vegetable bouillon cube

1. Preheat the oven to 375°F.

2. Line 2 baking sheets with parchment paper or silicone mats. Toss the cubed ciabatta on the baking sheet with 2 tablespoons of the oil, then spread them out evenly. Toss the cubed squash with 2 tablespoons of the oil, then spread evenly on the second prepared baking sheet. Bake the bread for 15 minutes and bake the squash for about 35 minutes, or until tender.

3. In a large cast-iron or oven-safe skillet, heat the remaining 1 tablespoon oil over medium-high heat. Add the onion, garlic, celery, and a dash of salt and cook until the onion is translucent, about 3 minutes. Stir in the mushrooms, sausages, sage, and rosemary and sauté until all the mushrooms release their juices and the vegetables are tender, about 10 minutes.

4. Add the toasted bread, roasted squash, 1 teaspoon salt, and the white pepper to the skillet and stir well to combine all the ingredients. Pour the stock over the stuffing and give it a little stir. Season to taste with more salt and white pepper.

5. Tightly cover the skillet with aluminum foil and bake for 30 minutes. Serve hot.

SOUTHERN *buddha* BOWL

• • • • • • •

serves **4**

I started making "Buddha bowls" for myself when I was a busy private chef in New York City. I'd spend my days cooking for clients and then find that I'd have no time or energy left to cook a wholesome meal for myself. Buddha bowls saved me, and they continue to be my go-to meal whenever I crave balance or need to save time in the kitchen. The term *Buddha bowl* comes from the Zen Buddhist tradition of consuming balanced meals in a mindful manner and the contents are inspired by Japanese macrobiotic cooking, which emphasizes balance of nutrients. This Buddha bowl joins eating with intention with nourishing ingredients common in the South.

If you're cooking for one or two people, I recommend prepping your ingredients on a free day so that you can quickly toss this bowl together when you're ready to eat it. Store the ingredients separately in stacking containers, or toss the ingredients together like a pilaf in a large container.

2 cups Veggie Mineral Stock (page 88) plus **1** teaspoon vegetable bouillon paste, or water

1 cup whole grain farro, soaked for **1** hour (pearled and semi-pearled farro may be used and do not require soaking)

1 ½ teaspoon sea salt

1 tablespoon grapeseed oil

1 cup whole or halved cherry tomatoes

2 jalapeño peppers, seeded and minced

2 cups fresh (from 2 large ears) or frozen corn kernels

1 bunch of collard greens, tough stems removed and leaves thinly sliced into ¼-inch ribbons (see Note on page **103**)

⅓ cup peach-miso vinaigrette (see page **211**), plus extra to top bowl

2 cups cooked butter beans or large lima beans (see page **125**) or 2 (15-ounce) cans, drained and rinsed

1 to 1 ½ cups Quick-Pickled Onions (page **75**)

1. In a medium pot, bring the stock to a boil and add the farro and salt. Reduce the heat to medium-low, partially cover the pot with a lid, and simmer for 30 to 45 minutes, or until tender.

2. In a large skillet, heat the oil over medium-high heat. Add the tomatoes, jalapeños, and corn and cook until they begin to char and are cooked through, about 15 minutes.

3. Place the collard ribbons in a large bowl, then add the ⅓ cup peach-miso vinaigrette. Using your clean hands, massage the collards for about 3 minutes, until tender.

4. Place ½ cup of each of the beans, farro, corn sauté, and collards in each bowl. Top with the pickled onions and peach-miso vinaigrette. Enjoy!

CORNBREAD
dressing

• • • • • • • •

serves **4 to 6**

The holidays are not the holidays without dressing, or stuffing, or filling—depending on where you're from. This tender, savory cornbread dressing is easy to make and even easier to devour. Next to Nana's Sweet Potato Pie (page 165), dressing is truly my favorite holiday food. If you're making this dressing with Smoky White Bean Sausages (page 59), they're best when made at least 8 hours in advance, which gives them a chance to firm to their ideal meaty texture. Store-bought vegan sausages will work here, too. This stuffing can be made up to 3 days in advance—just hold off on adding the stock until you're ready to bake.

1 tablespoon grapeseed oil

1 medium onion, thinly sliced

2 garlic cloves, minced

¾ to 1 cup diced celery

1 jalapeño pepper, seeded and minced

Sea salt

10 ounces baby bella mushrooms, minced (about 2 cups)

1 ½ teaspoons minced fresh rosemary

2 Smoky White Bean Sausages (page 59) or store-bought vegan sausages, diced

½ teaspoon freshly ground black pepper, plus more to taste

4½ cups Cornbread Croutons (page 77)

2 cups Veggie Mineral Stock (page 88), 2 cups water plus 1 vegetable bouillon cube, or 2 cups water plus 2 teaspoons vegetable bouillon paste

1. Preheat the oven to 375°F.

2. In a large cast-iron or oven-safe skillet, heat the oil over medium-high heat. Add the onion, garlic, celery, jalapeño, and a dash of salt and sauté until the onion is translucent, about 3 minutes. Add the mushrooms and rosemary to the skillet along with another dash of salt and cook until all the mushrooms start to release their liquid, about 5 minutes. Stir in the sausages and pepper and continue to cook until all the vegetables are tender. Add the croutons and stir well to combine all the ingredients. Pour the stock over the stuffing and give it another stir. Taste for seasoning and add more salt and pepper if desired.

3. Tightly cover the skillet with aluminum foil and bake for 25 minutes. Remove the foil and bake another 5 minutes, until the top browns slightly. Serve hot.

BOOTYLICIOUS GUMBO

• • • • • • •

serves **4**

The history of gumbo is as diverse as the southern Louisiana region where it has its roots. In West Africa, okra was called *ki ngombo* or *quingombo*. Some believe that the name made its way across the Atlantic with African slaves who brought okra along with them. Some believe that the word comes from the Choctaw word for dried sassafras leaves or filé—which is often used as a thickener in gumbo—*kombo*. Similarly, scholars disagree on the true origin of the dish. Is it from West Africans, Native Americans, or the French Acadian, aka Cajun, settlers? Most likely the dish is a melting pot with input from all these cultures.

My favorite way to make gumbo is with brown roux and tomatoes. A roux is a thickening stew or sauce base made with oil and flour. Gumbo roux tends to be cooked for longer so that it has more flavor than lighter roux. Tomatoes in gumbo are often reserved for seafood stews, but I've decided to bend the rules with my veggie-ful rendition. To make this gluten-free, use garbanzo flour for the roux and cooked chickpeas instead of the sausage.

¼ cup grapeseed oil

¼ cup unbleached all-purpose flour

1 large yellow onion, diced

3 garlic cloves, minced

2 celery stalks, diced (about 1 cup)

1 medium green bell pepper, diced

Sea salt

1 (14-ounce) can diced tomatoes

3 cups Veggie Mineral Stock (page 88) or 3 cups water plus 1 vegetable bouillon cube

1 bay leaf

1½ cups uncooked brown rice

2 Creole Red Bean Sausages (page 99) or store-bought smoked apple sage sausages, sliced ½ inch thick

1 tablespoon dried sage

1 teaspoon smoked paprika

1 teaspoon dried thyme

1 teaspoon dried rosemary

1 teaspoon fennel seeds

1 teaspoon freshly ground black pepper

¼ cup chopped fresh parsley, for garnish

1. Preheat a large dutch oven over medium heat. Add the oil, then sprinkle in the flour when the oil is hot. (Test the oil by dropping a pinch of flour in the oil; if it simmers, it is hot enough.) Toast the flour in the oil while stirring for a few minutes, until golden brown. Add the onion, garlic, celery, bell pepper, and a sprinkle of salt and stir. Sauté until the vegetables begin to soften, about 2 minutes. Add the diced tomatoes, stock, and bay leaf and stir well. Reduce the heat to medium-low and let simmer, uncovered, for 25 to 30 minutes (the longer it simmers, the thicker the gumbo).

2. Meanwhile, in a medium saucepan, bring the rice, 3 cups water, and a dash of salt to a boil. Reduce the heat to medium-low, partially cover with a lid, and simmer for about 30 minutes. Once finished, uncover and remove the pot from the heat.

3. Once the gumbo has thickened up, add the remaining ingredients. Cook for 8 minutes and adjust the salt to taste. Serve over brown rice and garnish with parsley.

PEACH-DATE BBQ *jackfruit* SLIDERS

• • • • • • •

makes **8 sliders**

Like other vegan meat substitutes, unripe (or green) jackfruit takes on the flavor of the seasonings you prepare it with. It's a perfect pair with rich sauces like the peach-date barbecue sauce used in this recipe. If you can't get your hands on unripened jackfruit, oyster mushrooms are a delicious and similar substitute.

To shred jackfruit, use the tines of a fork to pull apart its fibers. Use the same method to shred the tougher parts. Look for unripened jackfruit in a can at local Caribbean or Asian markets. If you cannot find it locally, check online, where there are many vendors.

2 (20-ounce) cans unripened green jackfruit in brine, drained and rinsed (see below)
2 cups Peach-Date BBQ Sauce (page 207)
8 vegan whole wheat slider buns
3 tablespoons vegan mayonnaise
1 cup Rainbow Root Slaw (page 79) or shredded red cabbage
¼ cup chopped fresh cilantro

1. Place the jackfruit in a large wide bowl, and use a fork to pull apart the fibers. The jackfruit should have a texture reminiscent of pulled chicken. Transfer the jackfruit to a large pot or skillet with a lid.

2. Pour the barbecue sauce over the jackfruit and stir to coat. Place the pot on the stove over medium-low heat and bring the jackfruit to a simmer. Cover the pot and cook for 20 minutes.

3. Toast the slider buns on both sides, then spread the vegan mayonnaise on the bottom half of each bun. Scoop about ½ cup of the barbecue jackfruit onto each bottom bun half. Top with slaw, a bit of cilantro, and the top bun half and serve.

HOLD UP . . . WHAT IS JACKFRUIT?

Jackfruit is a tropical fruit native to South and Southeast Asia. It's actually the world's largest tree fruit and can grow up to eighty pounds in size. Jackfruit comes two ways: ripe and unripened (or green). Ripe jackfruit is sweet and luscious, with a flavor like mango and pineapple (though it's not acidic). Unripened jackfruit has a stringy, meaty texture and is commonly used in vegetarian cooking as a meat substitute. I first tried unripe jackfruit in a curry while traveling in Bali. When it was served to me at a vegetarian restaurant I freaked, thinking I had been served chicken!

Jackfruit is high in vitamin C, vitamin B_6, potassium, and magnesium. It doesn't matter how it is cut, but make sure the can says the words *green* and *in brine*. A can of ripe jackfruit in syrup is useless for these recipes.

JACKFRUIT JAMBALAYA

• • • • • • •

serves **4**

Like gumbo, jambalaya is made a million and one ways, depending on the cook and the region. Jambalaya is a one-pot meal made with rice, vegetables—especially the Louisiana "Holy Trinity" of onions, celery, and green bell pepper—and meat or sausage. Some cooks use seafood, some use smoked sausage, and vegan cooks take it to the next level and use chickpeas, smoked tempeh, or meaty jackfruit. I love how the rice soaks up all the rich flavors of this dish, and it doesn't hurt that it's an easy one-pot meal.

3 tablespoons grapeseed oil

1 medium yellow onion, diced

2 garlic cloves, minced

3 celery stalks, chopped (1½ to 2 cups)

1 medium green bell pepper, chopped

1 (14-ounce) can diced tomatoes

1 cup uncooked brown rice

1½ cups cooked chickpeas (see page 125) or 1 (15-ounce) can, drained and rinsed

1 (20-ounce) can unripe green jackfruit in brine, shredded (see page 135)

3 cups Veggie Mineral Stock (page 88) or 3 cups water plus 1½ vegetable bouillon cubes

3 bay leaves

Freshly ground black pepper

1 tablespoon Creole Seasoning (page 36)

2 teaspoons vegan Worcestershire sauce

1 teaspoon Louisiana hot sauce, plus more for serving

Salt

¼ cup chopped fresh parsley, for garnish

1. Preheat a large dutch oven or heavy-bottomed pot over medium heat. Add the oil, followed by the onion, garlic, celery, and bell pepper. Sauté until the onion is translucent, about 3 minutes, then add the tomatoes, rice, chickpeas, and jackfruit. Stir well. Stir in the vegetable stock, bay leaves, and 1 teaspoon pepper. Cook with the lid ajar for 25 minutes, or until the rice is almost tender.

2. Add the Creole Seasoning, vegan Worcestershire sauce, and hot sauce and continue to cook until the rice is tender, about 15 minutes longer.

3. Taste for seasoning and add more salt and pepper if desired. Serve topped with fresh parsley and hot sauce.

LENTIL *loaf*

• • • • • • •

serves **4**

Meat loaf isn't a particularly Southern or soul food staple, but it is when my nana makes it. As the saying goes, she would put her foot in it—the result being the most delicious, comforting, and moist entrée. My version is just as satisfying but without harming any animals, and it's much healthier all around. I love serving this lentil loaf during the cooler months and at Thanksgiving dinner with Cider Cranberry Sauce (page 213) and/or Ooooh Mama Mushroom Gravy (page 205).

1 cup dried green lentils, sorted and rinsed

3 tablespoons ground flaxseed meal

2 tablespoons grapeseed oil

1 cup finely diced yellow onion

1 cup finely diced celery

3 garlic cloves, minced

1 cup shredded carrot

10 ounces baby bella mushrooms, minced (about 2 cups)

1 teaspoon dried thyme

1 teaspoon fennel seeds

2 tablespoons nutritional yeast

1 cup finely chopped toasted walnuts (see Note on page 164)

1 cup bread crumbs

1 ½ teaspoons salt, plus more to taste

1 teaspoon freshly ground black pepper, plus more to taste

Red chili flakes to taste

1. In a medium saucepan, bring 2½ cups water to a boil. Add the lentils, partially cover the pan with a lid, and cook until tender, 30 to 45 minutes, stirring halfway through. Drain and set aside.

2. In a small bowl, stir together the flaxseed meal and ½ cup water. Set it aside to thicken for at least 3 minutes.

3. In a large skillet, heat the oil over medium-high heat. Add the onion, celery, and garlic and sauté until the onion begins to soften, about 3 minutes. Add the shredded carrot and mushrooms, sautéing until the mushrooms begin to soften and release their liquid, about 5 minutes. Stir in the thyme and fennel seeds and continue to cook for 5 minutes.

4. Preheat the oven to 350°F. Line a loaf pan with parchment paper and set aside.

5. Once the mushrooms are soft, add the nutritional yeast, cooked lentils, flax mixture, walnuts, bread crumbs, salt, pepper, and chili flakes to the skillet. Stir well to combine all the ingredients. Taste for seasoning and add more salt and pepper if desired. The mixture should stick together, but if it doesn't, place about 1 cup of it into a food processor and pulse until it's a thick mush. Stir that back into the skillet.

6. Scoop the mixture into the prepared loaf pan and press firmly into the pan. Cover tightly with aluminum foil and bake for 30 minutes, or until the top of the loaf feels firm to the touch.

7. Let it cool for 10 to 20 minutes before slicing.

NEW ORLEANS— STYLE *red beans* & RICE

• • • • • • •

serves **6**

Red beans and rice have the magic to make you love Mondays. Down in New Orleans, it's an age-old tradition to eat this classic dish on the first day of the week. It's loaded with fiber, minerals, and B vitamins—the way to start the week off right! My vegan version of this New Orleans–style dish uses liquid smoke, smoked paprika, and Creole Red Bean Sausages (page 99) to achieve its traditional smoky richness.

4 tablespoons grapeseed oil

1 cup diced celery

1 medium yellow onion, diced

1 medium green bell pepper, diced

3 garlic cloves, diced

1 pound dried kidney beans, sorted, rinsed, and soaked for 8 hours

Pinch of salt

9 cups Veggie Mineral Stock (page 88) or 9 cups water plus 2 vegetable bouillon cubes

1 (4-inch) strip of kombu (optional)

4 bay leaves

2 teaspoons dried thyme

1 ½ cups uncooked brown rice

4 Creole Red Bean Sausages (page 99) or Smoky White Bean Sausages (page 59), sliced

3 teaspoons smoked paprika

1 teaspoon liquid smoke, or to taste

2 teaspoons Creole Seasoning (page 36)

1 cup chopped fresh parsley, for garnish

1. In a heavy-bottomed pot, heat 2 tablespoons of the oil over medium-high heat. Add the celery, onion, bell pepper, and garlic and sauté until the onion is translucent, about 3 minutes. Add the beans, salt, and stock. Bring to a boil, then add the kombu (if using), bay leaves, and thyme. Reduce the heat to medium-low and simmer for 60 to 90 minutes, checking halfway through to skim off any foam that may form on the top. The beans should be tender but still maintain their shape when done.

2. While the beans are cooking, make your rice following the package instructions. Set aside.

3. To prepare your vegan sausages, in a large skillet, heat the remaining 2 tablespoons oil over medium-high heat. Add the sliced sausages and cook on each side until they begin to brown, about 3 minutes each side.

4. When the beans have finished cooking (taste a bean to make sure it is tender), remove them from the heat and stir in the paprika, liquid smoke, and Creole Seasoning. Stir in the vegan sausage.

5. Serve immediately over the rice and garnish with the parsley.

BOURBON BBQ TEMPEH
sandwiches

• • • • • • •

serves **4**

Forget about the animal products! Instead, throw some delicious and toothsome barbecued tempeh on the grill. This fermented soybean cake has lots of nutrition, glorious texture, and an incredible ability to soak up and balance the flavors of any marinade. The longer you cook it, the more tender and delicious it gets. I love to serve these sliders at family gatherings with the Coconut Collard Salad (page 74), Hickory Baked Beans (page 114), Late-Summer Sangria (page 200), and No-Bake Stone Fruit Cobbler (page 171) for dessert. Eat up, y'all!

NOTE: Some brands and varieties of tempeh tend to be denser and firmer. With those brands, you may want to steam your tempeh for about 15 minutes before using it in this recipe to allow it to soak up the sauce better.

2 (8-ounce) packages tempeh

2 cups Bourbon BBQ Sauce (page 208)

4 vegan soft burger buns

¼ cup vegan mayonnaise

½ cup Quick-Pickled Onions (page 75)

4 romaine lettuce leaves, chopped

1. Cut a block of tempeh crosswise in half to make 2 squares. Cut each half down the middle to make 2 thinner square pieces. Repeat with the second package of tempeh. You should end up with 8 thin squares.

2. Place the tempeh slices in a large saucepan over medium heat and cover with the barbecue sauce. Stir well and bring the sauce to a simmer. Cover, reduce to medium-low heat, and cook for 20 minutes. The tempeh will absorb some of the sauce. Check it every 5 minutes to stir and make sure it isn't burning. Reduce the heat to low if necessary.

3. Toast the burger buns on both sides, then spread 1 tablespoon of the vegan mayonnaise on the bottom half of each bun. Carefully remove the tempeh and place 2 slices on each bottom bun half. Top each piece of tempeh with a few tablespoons of the pickled onions, chopped romaine, then the top bun half, and serve.

FRIED
shallots

● ● ● ● ● ● ●

makes about 1½ cups

I first tried fried shallots while visiting
my friend Karen Waddell at her organic
farm compound just upriver from Ubud
in Bali. They were fried to perfection
in the outdoor kitchen's huge clay pot.
Since then, I've sought out dishes with
them at restaurants and will substitute
them in any recipe calling for fried
onions. Shallots have a sweeter flavor
than most onions and to me seem like
the love child of an onion and garlic.
Add fried shallots to just about any
savory dish—including salads, soups,
and sandwiches.

2 cups coconut or grapeseed oil

6 large shallots, thinly sliced

½ teaspoon salt

1. Double-line a large plate with paper towels and keep
nearby.

2. In a saucepan, heat the oil over high heat. When the
oil is hot (see the Note on page 107), add the shallots and
fry for about 10 minutes, or until they are golden brown.
Use a handled sieve or slotted spoon to transfer the fried
shallots to the prepared plate. Sprinkle salt over the
shallots as they cool. They will become crisper as they
continue to cool.

3. Store fried shallots in an airtight container in the
refrigerator for up to 7 days.

OYSTER
mushroom
ÉTOUFFÉE

• • • • • • • •

serves **4**

Étouffée means "smothered," and that's exactly what this dish is. A smothered mess of luscious oyster mushrooms, vegetables, and spices in a delicious roux-based sauce over tender boiled rice. Like most southern Louisiana dishes, traditional étouffée is made with seafood—crawfish or shrimp—to be exact. Oyster mushrooms, however, are a fantastic whole food alternative to shellfish. They're rich in cancer-fighting antioxidants and anti-inflammatory compounds, making them just as good for our health as they are for our taste buds.

3 tablespoons grapeseed or coconut oil

3 tablespoons unbleached all-purpose flour

1 small yellow onion, diced

2 garlic cloves, minced

1 small green bell pepper, diced

2 celery stalks, diced (about 1 cup)

½ teaspoon salt

½ (14-ounce) can diced tomatoes (about 1 cup)

2½ cups Veggie Mineral Stock (page 88) or
    2½ cups water plus 1 vegetable bouillon cube

1 bay leaf

1 teaspoon dulse seaweed flakes

1 tablespoon Creole Seasoning (page 36)

3 teaspoons Old Bay seasoning, plus more to taste

1 pound fresh oyster mushrooms, roughly chopped
    (about 2 cups)

2 cups cooked brown rice

1 lemon

½ cup chopped fresh parsley, for serving

1. Preheat a large dutch oven or heavy-bottomed pot over medium heat. Add the oil, then sprinkle in the flour when the oil is hot. (Test the oil by dropping a pinch of flour in the oil; if it simmers, it is hot enough.) Toast the flour in the oil, stirring for a few minutes until it turns golden brown. Add the onion, garlic, bell pepper, celery, and salt and stir. Sauté on medium until the onion is translucent, about 3 minutes. Add the diced tomatoes, stock, bay leaf, dulse, Creole Seasoning, and Old Bay seasoning. Stir well and bring the pot to a simmer. Add the mushrooms and continue to simmer for 20 minutes until they become tender.

2. Taste for seasoning and add more Old Bay seasoning if desired. Serve over rice with a squeeze of lemon juice and garnished with parsley.

BLACK-EYED PEA POTPIE

· · · · · · · ·

serves 4 to 6

Pot pie isn't a particularly Southern dish, but it sure is an American classic. This version adds a little Southern charm with the addition of black-eyed peas and jalapeño peppers. If you're yearning for a meatier addition, throw in about 1 cup store-bought vegan chicken strips when you add the beans.

2 tablespoons coconut or grapeseed oil

1 medium yellow onion, diced

1 cup diced celery

2 garlic cloves, minced

1 jalapeño pepper, seeded and diced

1 teaspoon salt, plus more as needed

1 cup diced carrot

1 small unpeeled sweet potato, cut into ¼-inch cubes

1 small unpeeled red or Yukon Gold potato, cut into ¼-inch cubes

3 cups Veggie Mineral Stock (page 88) or 3 cups water plus 1 vegetable bouillon cube

1 cup fresh or frozen green peas

1½ cups cooked black-eyed peas (see page 125) or 1 (15-ounce) can, drained and rinsed

1 teaspoon white pepper

½ teaspoon dried thyme

½ teaspoon celery seeds

½ teaspoon fennel seeds

½ teaspoon dried sage

2 Flaky Double Piecrusts (page 166) or 2 9-inch store-bought vegan crusts

2 tablespoons potato starch

2 tablespoons soy sauce

1. In a large dutch oven or heavy-bottomed pot, heat the oil over medium heat. Add the onion, celery, garlic, jalapeño, and a sprinkle of salt. Sauté until the onion is translucent, about 3 minutes. Add the carrot, sweet potato, and red potato. Add 2 cups of the stock and simmer for 10 minutes, until the potatoes begin to soften. Add the peas, black-eyed peas, white pepper, thyme, celery seeds, fennel seeds, sage, and 1 teaspoon salt (skip this if using salted vegetable bouillon). Cook for 10 minutes longer.

2. Preheat the oven to 400°F.

3. Prepare your piecrusts. If you are using a frozen store-bought piecrust for the topping, remove it from the freezer and allow it to soften on the kitchen counter.

4. In a small bowl, stir together the remaining 1 cup stock with the potato starch, making sure to break up any clumps. Stir the starch mixture into the pot. Reduce the heat to low, add the soy sauce, and continue stirring until the vegetable mixture thickens, about 1 minute. Remove it from the heat and season to taste with more salt, if desired.

5. Scoop the vegetable stew into the bottom crust in a pie dish. Cover it with the top crust and crimp the edges to seal them together. Cut a few slits in the top of the pie to vent steam. Bake for 30 minutes, or until the piecrust becomes golden brown. Let the pot pie cool for at least 10 minutes before serving.

SWEET POTATO *green bean* CASSEROLE

• • • • • • •

serves **6**

Southerners love their casseroles, but I was never a fan of the heavy cheese-laden varieties. I haven't been diagnosed as lactose intolerant, but I'm sure I am, and my intuition has always steered me clear of anything containing more than a couple ounces of cheese.

Becoming vegan opened my eyes to the possibility of making rich, comforting, and cheesy dishes without a drop of dairy. I think dairy-free casseroles taste fresher and let the flavors and textures of the vegetables stand out and be appreciated.

This green bean casserole takes advantage of the cream-making power of cauliflower, white beans, and nutritional yeast for a decadent yet 100 percent healthy sauce. The thin layer of sweet potato at the bottom of the casserole is a nice starchy and sweet addition to this savory dish.

3 medium sweet potatoes, peeled and sliced into ¼-inch-thick medallions

4 tablespoons grapeseed oil

Salt

1 small head of cauliflower, roughly chopped into small pieces

1 small yellow onion, diced

10 ounces baby bella mushrooms (about 2 cups), thinly sliced

1½ cups cooked cannellini beans or 1 (15-ounce can), drained and rinsed

1 cup plain unsweetened soy milk or other nondairy milk

2 teaspoons vegetable bouillon paste or 1 vegetable bouillon cube

1 teaspoon porcini powder (optional)

1 teaspoon dried thyme

1 teaspoon *ume* plum vinegar or lemon juice

¼ cup nutritional yeast

1 teaspoon freshly ground black pepper

1 pound fresh green beans or 1 (14-ounce) bag frozen green beans, thawed and cut into 1-inch pieces

1 cup Fried Shallots (page 143)

1. Preheat the oven to 375°F. Line a baking sheet with parchment paper or a silicone mat and keep nearby.

2. In a 9 × 9-inch baking or casserole dish, toss the sweet potato medallions with 1 tablespoon of the oil. Arrange them evenly in the bottom of the dish and sprinkle with salt. The sweet potatoes will overlap. Set aside while you prepare the cauliflower.

3. Place the chopped cauliflower on the prepared baking sheet. Drizzle 2 tablespoons of the oil over the cauliflower, then evenly arrange the pieces over the sheet. Add a sprinkle of salt. Place both the sweet potatoes and cauliflower in the oven and roast for 30 minutes, or until the vegetables are tender.

4. In a large saucepan, heat the remaining 1 tablespoon oil over medium-high heat. Add the onion and sauté until it is translucent, about 3 minutes. Stir in the mushrooms and beans. Reduce the heat to medium-low and continue to cook until the mushrooms start to release their juices and become tender, about 10 minutes. Add 1 cup water, the soy milk, bouillon paste, porcini powder, and thyme. Partially cover the pan with a lid and simmer for another 10 minutes. Add three quarters of the roasted cauliflower, the vinegar, nutritional yeast, and ½ teaspoon salt. Cook for 5 more minutes.

5. Remove the pan from the heat and use a handheld immersion blender to puree about two thirds of the mixture. If you do not have an immersion blender, allow the mixture to cool until it's safe to transfer three quarters of it to a blender to puree. Return the pan to the heat and add the black pepper and green beans. Stir well to combine.

6. Spoon the green bean mixture over the top of the roasted sweet potatoes in the casserole dish. Top the dish with the remaining roasted cauliflower. Bake for 20 minutes and serve hot, topped with the fried shallots.

CAJUN BLACKENED *tofu* SANDWICH

• • • • • • • •

serves **4**

My mom is the blackened-seasoning queen! She's not a big fan of cooking, but she knows a few shortcuts to make a superquick meal taste good. Rule 1: use a flavorful spice blend. Blackened seasoning is a staple of Cajun cuisine and is most often used on fish. The technique entails pan-frying the spice-coated food, in this case tofu, until the spices char and create a crispy and flavorful coating.

This recipe does require you to marinate the tofu overnight in a beer-based sauce, but that takes just a couple of minutes to throw together before you go to bed. Even my mom can appreciate this easy recipe!

TOFU MARINADE

1 cup beer (I prefer a golden ale but use whatever vegan beer you like)

1 tablespoon dulse seaweed flakes

¼ cup tamari soy sauce

1 (12-ounce) block of extra-firm tofu, drained and sliced ½ inch thick (you should have around 6 slices)

1 tablespoon coconut, canola, or grapeseed oil

¼ to ½ cup Creole Seasoning (page 36) or store-bought salt-free Cajun blackened seasoning

FOR SERVING

4 vegan soft burger buns or whole wheat bread

¼ cup vegan mayonnaise

1 cup Spicy Peach-Tomatillo Salsa (page 212)

1 cup microgreens (optional)

1. Make the marinade: In a small bowl, whisk together the beer, dulse, and tamari.

2. Place the tofu slices in a storage container or quart-size plastic zip bag and cover with the marinade. Marinate in the refrigerator overnight, or at least 6 hours.

3. In a large cast-iron or nonstick skillet, heat the oil over medium-high heat. Remove the tofu slices from the refrigerator, place on a plate, and sprinkle 1 tablespoon of blackened seasoning on all sides of each tofu slice. Working in batches if necessary, place the seasoned tofu slices in the hot skillet and pan-fry for about 3 minutes each side, until the seasoning has blackened and seeped into the tofu.

4. Toast the burger buns on both sides. To serve, spread 1 tablespoon vegan mayonnaise on the bottom half of each bun. Carefully remove the blackened tofu from the skillet and place a slice on top of each bottom bun half. Top each piece of tofu with ¼ cup salsa and microgreens (if using), then the top bun half, and serve.

spicy fried CAULIFLOWER "CHICKEN"

• • • • • • •

serves 4

1 cup unbleached all-purpose flour

1 tablespoon arrowroot powder or cornstarch

½ teaspoon salt

½ teaspoon cayenne pepper

½ teaspoon white pepper

½ teaspoon onion powder

½ teaspoon garlic powder

½ teaspoon sweet or smoked paprika

¼ teaspoon Old Bay seasoning

1 tablespoon nutritional yeast

⅓ cup hot sauce

¼ cup plain unsweetened soy milk or other nondairy milk

1 tablespoon Dijon mustard

5 cups safflower or other neutral oil, for frying

1 large head of cauliflower, cut into large florets

I stopped eating chicken the summer of 2008, and even back then, long before I had any inkling that I would one day become vegan, I was so proud of my accomplishment. Before then I loved chicken, especially fried, but I had gladly accepted that I would never experience anything like it ever again. Lo and behold, the best fried "chicken" I've had is made with cauliflower. I'm not sure who the first person was to fry up a piece of cauliflower with a fried chicken batter, but I thank that person every time I make this dish. After experimenting with different batter seasonings for actual chicken, I landed on the recipe below. Serve with a plate of Tender Mess o' Collard Greens (page 103), Georgia Watermelon & Peach Salad (page 84), and Harlem Caviar: Black-eyed Pea Salad (page 85).

1. In a medium bowl, combine the flour, arrowroot powder, salt, cayenne, white pepper, onion powder, garlic powder, paprika, Old Bay seasoning, and nutritional yeast.

2. In another mixing bowl, combine the hot sauce, soy milk, and Dijon mustard and whisk until creamy.

3. In a large dutch oven or fryer, heat the oil to 350°F (see Note on page 107). Double-line a large plate with paper towels and keep nearby.

4. Use 1 hand to dip a cauliflower floret into the wet mixture, then drop it into the flour mixture. Use your dry hand to coat it completely. Dip it back into the wet mixture and again into the dry mixture, keeping 1 hand devoted to wet and 1 to dry.

5. Carefully lower the twice-coated floret into the hot oil. Repeat with the remaining cauliflower until you can't fit any more into the dutch oven. Do not overcrowd. Fry for 4 to 5 minutes, until the pieces are golden. Transfer the fried cauliflower to the prepared plate and continue to fry the remaining cauliflower. Serve hot.

good luck BLACK-EYED PEAS

• • • • • • • •

serves **6**

One should never skip a plate of black-eyed peas and collards on New Year's Day. According to Southern lore, eating black-eyed peas on the first day of the year brings luck in the coming year. Some folks will cook their pot of beans with a penny or a dime, and whoever gets the bowl with the metal jewel is said to have the best luck of all in the coming year. This tradition has fascinating and surprising origins. Sephardic Jewish people, who ate black-eyed peas during Rosh Hashanah (the Jewish New Year), brought the tradition to the American South in the 1700s. Though black-eyed peas were first cultivated in West Africa and probably made their way to the United States on board slave vessels, this legume has been widely used in Egypt and the Middle East for centuries.

Depending on how wet you like your beans, add 5 to 6 cups of water (6 cups for soupier beans). Don't forget the Skillet Cornbread (page 102).

¼ cup grapeseed oil

1 medium yellow onion, diced

1 large red bell pepper, diced

1 jalapeño pepper, seeded and diced

1 cup diced celery

3 garlic cloves, minced

1 pound dried black-eyed peas, sorted, rinsed, and soaked for 8 hours

6 cups Veggie Mineral Stock (page 88), 6 cups water plus 6 teaspoons vegetable bouillon paste, or 6 cups water plus 2 vegetable bouillon cubes

1 bay leaf

2 teaspoons smoked paprika

1 tablespoon liquid smoke

1 tablespoon soy sauce

1 teaspoon freshly ground black pepper

½ teaspoon cayenne pepper, or to taste

1. In a large dutch oven, heat the oil over medium-high heat. Add the onion, bell pepper, jalapeño, celery, and garlic and sauté until the onion is translucent, about 3 minutes. Add the black-eyed peas, stock, and bay leaf. Cover and bring to a light boil. Reduce the heat to medium-low and simmer for about 40 minutes, or until the beans are tender and the stock has thickened. Stir in the paprika, liquid smoke, soy sauce, pepper, and cayenne.

2. Remove from the heat and let the beans cool a bit. Serve with collard greens and cornbread.

smoky BLACK-EYED PEA CAKES

. . . .

makes 8 small cakes

I love anything with black-eyed peas, and these cakes are one of my favorite ways to eat my favorite beans. They're perfectly crispy on the outside with a soft, flavorful interior. Serve these cakes with the Coconut Collard Salad (page 74) and Pecan Muhammara (page 214) for a truly spectacular, healthy feast or enjoy alone.

This recipe calls for two types of bread crumbs: panko bread crumbs, which are larger flakes, and normal fine bread crumbs, which are closer to a powder. Panko bread crumbs go into the batter, and I use a mixture of both for the breading to get the perfect crispy texture. If you'd rather keep it simple, just use panko.

1 tablespoon finely ground flaxseed

1 ½ cups cooked black-eyed peas (see page 125) or 1 (15-ounce) can, drained and rinsed

¼ fine or medium-ground cornmeal

¼ cup plus 2 tablespoons panko bread crumbs

½ cup minced yellow onion

2 garlic cloves, minced

1 jalapeño pepper, minced (remove the seeds if you don't want them to be spicy)

1 teaspoon smoked paprika

1 teaspoon dried thyme

1 teaspoon ground cumin

1 teaspoon sea salt

1 teaspoon apple cider vinegar

2 tablespoons bread crumbs

Vegetable oil, for frying

1. In a small bowl, stir together the flaxseed meal and 2 tablespoons of water. Set it aside to thicken for at least 3 minutes.

2. Place the black-eyed peas, cornmeal, ¼ cup panko, onion, garlic, jalapeño, paprika, thyme, cumin, salt, and vinegar in a food processor. Scrape in the flaxseed meal mixture and pulse until combined. Don't overprocess it; the black-eyed peas should retain a little texture.

3. In a small bowl, stir together the remaining 2 tablespoons panko and the bread crumbs.

4. Form the mixture into 8 small cakes about 2 inches wide. Gently dip each side into the bread crumb mixture to coat and set them on a large plate.

5. Double-line another large plate with paper towels and keep nearby.

6. In a large cast-iron skillet or frying pan, heat about ¼ inch oil to 350°F (see Note on page 107). Working in batches if necessary, fry the black-eyed pea cakes on each side for 4 to 5 minutes, until golden brown. Set them on the prepared plate.

SWEET POTATO *burgers*

• • • • • • • •

makes 8 burgers

I cannot think of a food more American than the cheeseburger, except maybe the veggie burger. Since their emergence in the 1980s, veggie burgers have only gotten more delicious, interesting, diverse, and popular. Since I'm a Southern girl, my favorite veggie burger has sweet potato as its prime ingredient. These burgers are great on the grill, pan-fried, or baked in the oven. Try them with Red Pepper Aioli (page 209) and Quick-Pickled Onions (page 75) on a classic sesame bun.

BURGERS

½ large red bell pepper, roughly chopped

½ medium red onion, roughly chopped

1 (15-ounce) can chickpeas, drained and rinsed

1 cup (packed) cilantro, parsley, or a mix of the two

3 garlic cloves

½ cup almonds

2 tablespoons ground cumin, plus more to taste

3 teaspoons ground coriander, plus more to taste

2 teaspoons smoked paprika, plus more to taste

2½ teaspoons sea salt, plus more to taste

1 teaspoon freshly ground black pepper, plus more to taste

1 cup mashed sweet potato (from 1 baked medium sweet potato)

¾ cup quick-cooking oats

FOR SERVING

8 vegan sesame buns

½ cup Red Pepper Aioli (page 209)

¼ cup Quick-Pickled Onions (page 75)

1 handful of chopped romaine lettuce, spinach, or arugula

1. In a food processor, pulse and finely chop the bell pepper and red onion. Scrape the chopped veggies into a large bowl.

2. Place the chickpeas and cilantro in the food processor and blend until the chickpeas have a thick, mealy texture. Scrape into the bowl with the peppers and onions.

3. Place the garlic, almonds, cumin, coriander, paprika, salt, and pepper in the food processor and blend until the almonds have a crumbly texture. Scrape into the bowl. Add the sweet potato and oats and stir well to combine the ingredients. Taste for seasoning and adjust as desired.

4. Preheat the oven to 375°F. Line a baking sheet with parchment paper and keep nearby.

5. Scoop about ¾ cup of the mixture into your hands, form it into a tight patty, and place on the prepared baking sheet. If the patty doesn't hold well when shaped, it's probably because it is too wet. As a remedy, place the mixture in the refrigerator for 1 hour to firm up. (This scenario is unlikely, but it could happen if you overprocess the bell pepper and onion.) Repeat with the remaining batter, spacing the patties 2 inches apart on the baking sheet. Bake for 40 minutes, or until cooked through and browned on the side facing down. Alternatively, grill or pan-fry them on each side for 5 minutes.

6. Let the patties cool for at least 15 minutes before trying to remove them from the baking sheet with a spatula or your hands.

7. Toast the sesame buns on both sides. To serve, spread about ½ tablespoon aioli on the bottom half of each bun. Place a burger on each bottom bun half and top with pickled onions, lettuce, and the remaining bun half.

SWEETS & DRINKS

STEP INTO ANY SOUTHERN HOUSEHOLD AND you'll find that sweets are an important part of the region's cuisine. No meal is complete without a slice of Georgia Pecan Pie (page 164), Cream Cheese Pound Cake (page 174), a bowl of warm and tender Date Rice Pudding (page 167), or a helping of fresh fruit. Like other soul food, sweets represent love, family, and tradition.

Luckily we don't have to rely on animal products for great Southern baking. We can bring trademark desserts to life by replacing eggs with ground flaxseed, milk with nondairy substitutes, and butter with vegan butter (even for flaky piecrusts). Yes, even dairy butter can be replaced! You won't find an ounce of animal products in these desserts, but you will find a whole lot of sweet soulful goodness.

If you are looking for healthier desserts, don't miss the No-Bake Stone Fruit Cobbler (page 171), Strawberry Shortcake (page 172), Sweet Potato–Tahini Cookies (page 180), Caramelized Coconut Grilled Peaches (page 182), and No-Bake Sweet Potato Gingerbread Bars (page 188). The best way to reduce your intake of processed sugar is to replace it with more wholesome sweeteners like the ones found in these guilt-free sweets.

This chapter also features my favorite Southern-inspired drinks and cocktails, because I couldn't have a cookbook without sweet tea (see Summer Molasses Iced Tea on page 192). When it's hot outside, there's nothing more refreshing than a cold glass of something Southern. These drinks and cocktails put a spin on soulful classics. The cocktails also can be made virgin, and the refreshments can be spiked.

CARDAMOM
apple pie

• • • • • • •

makes 1 9-inch pie

Just a dash of cardamom elevates this traditional apple pie to new heights. Though cardamom is not a Southern spice, it plays well with cinnamon, nutmeg, and allspice and adds a cozy Southern charm to this dessert. Cardamom is actually native to South Asia and is commonly used in cuisine from that region, most notably in chai. Cardamom is pricey, and a little goes a very long way. I like to purchase the seeds and grind them myself for the freshest taste.

8 baking apples, such as Granny Smith, cored, peeled, and thinly sliced about ⅛ inch thick

1 ½ tablespoons freshly squeezed lemon juice

⅓ cup brown sugar

⅓ cup cane sugar

1 teaspoon ground cinnamon

½ teaspoon freshly grated nutmeg

¼ teaspoon allspice

½ teaspoon ground cardamom

¼ teaspoon ground ginger

¼ teaspoon salt

2 tablespoons potato starch

¼ cup apple cider or water

1 recipe Flaky Double Piecrust (page 166) or 2 store-bought vegan piecrusts

2 tablespoons solid coconut oil

1. Preheat the oven to 400°F.

2. Place the sliced apples in a large bowl, add the lemon juice, and toss to coat. Transfer them to a large saucepan and place over medium heat. Add the sugars, cinnamon, nutmeg, allspice, cardamom, ginger, and salt. Stir well. Bring to a simmer and cook for 10 minutes, or until the apples soften.

3. In a small bowl, stir together the potato starch and cider until the starch dissolves. Pour it into the apples and stir as it thickens. Remove from the heat.

4. Pour the apples evenly into the bottom piecrust. Top the apples with small pieces of the coconut oil. Top with the other piecrust and crimp the edges. Make slits in the crust to release steam as it bakes. Bake for 45 minutes, or until the top of the piecrust turns golden and the edges are slightly browned. If the edges are browning too quickly, wrap them in aluminum foil.

5. Remove the pie from the oven and let cool for 1 hour before serving.

GEORGIA PECAN
PIE, page 164

NANA'S SWEET
POTATO PIE,
page 165

GEORGIA
pecan pie

• • • • • • •

makes 1 9-inch pie

The secret to a sublime vegan pecan pie is none other than sweet potato! It replaces the egg in this recipe and keeps the syrupy pecan filling gooey and light. No one knows for sure who created the first pecan pie, but it's been a staple on Thanksgiving tables in the South since the 1800s. This delectable autumn pie should be eaten with Bourbon Vanilla Ice Cream (page 184).

NOTE: Toasting nuts and seeds is the best way to deepen their flavor and make them even more delicious. My favorite way to do this is in the oven. Preheat the oven to 350°F and line a baking sheet with parchment paper. Spread the nuts evenly onto the prepared baking sheet and roast for 5 to 10 minutes. Pecans and walnuts usually toast for about 8 minutes. Nuts burn easily, so be sure to set a timer for yourself.

Another way to toast them is in a dry skillet. Spread the nuts evenly onto a skillet over medium heat. When the nuts start to toast (you will smell them), shake the pan to let them toast evenly. Do this for about 5 minutes. With both toasting methods, you'll know the nuts are done when they have darkened slightly.

1 cup mashed sweet potato (from 1 baked medium sweet potato)

3 tablespoons arrowroot powder or cornstarch

¼ cup vegan butter

¼ cup plain unsweetened soy milk or other nondairy milk

1 cup cane sugar

½ cup light or dark corn syrup

2 teaspoons pure vanilla extract

¼ teaspoon sea salt

2 cups toasted pecans (see Note)

½ recipe Flaky Double Piecrust (page 166) or 1 store-bought vegan crust

1. Preheat the oven to 350°F.

2. In a large bowl, combine the mashed sweet potato and arrowroot powder and set aside.

3. In a medium saucepan over medium heat, combine the vegan butter, soy milk, sugar, corn syrup, vanilla, and salt. Melt the vegan butter and combine the ingredients. Stir constantly as the mixture begins to boil. Let boil for about 3 minutes, then remove from the heat.

4. Slowly pour the sugar mixture into the bowl with the sweet potato and arrowroot and whisk well to combine.

5. Spread the toasted pecans in the bottom of the piecrust. Pour the filling over the pecans and shake a couple times to set the whole filling. Bake for 45 to 50 minutes, until the edges are golden brown.

6. Remove the pie from the oven and let it cool for an hour or so before serving. Store leftover pie in the refrigerator for up to 5 days.

NANA'S SWEET POTATO *pie*

· · · · · · · ·

makes 2 9-inch pies

3 cups mashed sweet potato (around 4 baked medium sweet potatoes)

1 cup mashed butternut squash (see Note)

1 cup plain unsweetened soy milk or other nondairy milk

½ cup light brown sugar

½ cup cane sugar

¼ cup arrowroot powder

2 teaspoons ground cinnamon

½ teaspoon freshly grated nutmeg

½ teaspoon salt

⅜ teaspoon ground cloves

1 teaspoon pure vanilla extract

1 recipe Flaky Double Piecrust (page 166) or 2 store-bought vegan crusts

There is literally nothing better than a perfectly sweet and slightly firm slice of sweet potato pie. It's my favorite dessert and has been for as long as I can remember. My nana makes a bunch of them every year for Thanksgiving and Christmas and has always reserved a whole entire pie just for me. The key to a great sweet potato pie is the flavor and texture. Flavor is easy to replicate without using animal products, but the texture took me a couple of years to nail down. The secret replacement for eggs in this recipe is butternut squash—it firms when chilled—and arrowroot powder. For the tastiest and best-textured pie, make sure to use home-baked sweet potato and butternut squash. Canned squash tends to have too much liquid and just doesn't firm up as well.

1. Preheat the oven to 350°F.

2. Place the mashed sweet potato, mashed squash, soy milk, brown sugar, cane sugar, arrowroot, cinnamon, nutmeg, salt, cloves, and vanilla in a blender and puree until smooth. Scrape the filling into the crusts and bake for 50 minutes, or until the top of the pie is dry to the touch.

3. Remove from the oven and let cool for at least 30 minutes, then set in the fridge to chill for a few more hours or overnight. Serve chilled or at room temperature. The pie can be stored in a covered pie dish for up to 5 days.

NOTE: To make mashed squash, halve a large butternut squash (around 3 pounds) and scoop out the seeds. Coat the squash halves with 1 teaspoon grapeseed oil and place them cut side up on a baking sheet lined with parchment paper. Bake at 375°F for 45 minutes, or until tender. Once it is cool enough to handle, use a spoon to scoop out the flesh of one of the squash halves (reserve the other half for another use) into a small bowl. Mash the squash well with a fork. You should have about 1 cup.

FLAKY DOUBLE *piecrust*

• • • • • • • •

makes 2 9-inch crusts

Everything you want in a piecrust without an ounce of butter! Like your grandma's piecrusts, this one uses the perfect combination of fat, ice-cold water, and flour to achieve flaky perfection. This recipe makes two crusts that can be used immediately or frozen for later.

2½ cups all-purpose flour, plus more for dusting

1 teaspoon salt

1 tablespoon sugar

½ cup plus 2 tablespoons vegan butter or vegan shortening, cubed

½ cup plus 2 to 4 tablespoons ice-cold water

1. In a medium bowl, whisk together the flour, salt, and sugar.

2. Add the cubes of vegan butter and use a pastry cutter to incorporate it into the flour until the mixture resembles coarse pea-size meal. Slowly add the water, 2 tablespoons at a time, and stir with a wooden spoon or your hands. Once the dough begins to hold together, form it into 2 balls. Flatten them a bit (this will make it easier to roll out later), wrap them in plastic wrap or parchment paper, and flatten them to about 1-inch thick disks within the wrap. Place in the refrigerator for at least 1 hour.

3. Remove the chilled pie dough from the fridge. Let it sit on the counter for 10 minutes to soften.

4. Flour a clean, smooth stone surface and place one of the dough balls down onto it. (If you don't have a stone surface, spread parchment paper over the surface you do have.) Use a floured rolling pin to roll out the dough into a flat circle. Roll the pin away from you and rotate the dough after each roll to prevent it from sticking to the counter. It should be about ⅛ inch thick and wide enough to comfortably fit over your pie dish with at least 2 inches of extra space along the sides.

5. Remove the piecrust from the surface by very gently rolling it around the rolling pin, then guide it evenly over a 9-inch pie dish. Carefully press it into the dish and up the sides. Place in the refrigerator.

6. Repeat the rolling-out steps with the remaining dough for a double crust or for 2 separate pies. If you are using the second crust as a pie topping, wait until the pie is filled and ready to top before rolling it out.

7. Unbaked piecrusts can be stored in the freezer for up to 2 months.

DATE RICE *pudding*

● ● ● ● ● ● ●

serves 6

The most-comforting-dessert award goes to this hot and creamy rice pudding. Don't make this without guests around to help you eat it or you'll end up devouring the whole pot yourself. I prefer dates in my rice pudding because they are caramel-y and blend exceedingly well with the coconut and spices. Most Southern cooks include raisins or no dried fruit at all. If possible, use freshly ground nutmeg in this recipe (and all others that call for it)—there's nothing better!

½ cup white basmati rice

1 (14-ounce) can full-fat coconut milk

¼ cup sugar

2 tablespoons arrowroot powder or cornstarch

¼ teaspoon ground cinnamon, plus more for serving

¼ teaspoon freshly grated nutmeg

⅛ teaspoon allspice

1 teaspoon pure vanilla extract

1 cup plain unsweetened soy milk or other nondairy milk

¼ cup chopped pitted dates

1. In a medium saucepan, bring 1 cup of water to a boil. Add the rice, partially cover it with a lid, and reduce the heat to medium. Simmer until the rice has absorbed all the liquid, about 20 minutes.

2. Preheat the oven to 350°F.

3. In a standing mixer with the whisk attachment, beat together the coconut milk and sugar on medium-high speed until fluffy. (Alternatively, you can use a hand mixer.) Beat in the arrowroot, cinnamon, nutmeg, allspice, and vanilla. Slowly pour in the soy milk and beat until well combined, about 30 seconds. Stir in the cooked rice and chopped dates until well incorporated. Scrape the mixture into an 8 × 8-inch baking dish and bake for 30 minutes (or 40 minutes if you like a drier rice pudding). The rice mixture will be very liquid-y, but don't worry. It will soak up the liquid and become very creamy while it cooks.

4. Remove from the oven and let the rice pudding cool for about 5 minutes. Serve with a dash of cinnamon on top. Keep leftover rice pudding in the refrigerator for up to 2 days.

NO-BAKE STONE FRUIT
COBBLER, page 171

STRAWBERRY
SHORTCAKE,
page 172

GINGER-KISSED
PEACH COBBLER,
page 170

GINGER-KISSED *peach* COBBLER

• • • • • • •

serves **4** to **6**

In the fall and winter we eat sweet potato and pecan pies, in the spring we have strawberry shortcake, and in the summer we eat peach cobbler. When you're driving through Georgia in the summer, you'll pass little farm stands advertising fresh and juicy peaches. If the peaches are really good, you may even smell them before you see a sign. With such an abundance of peaches screaming to be devoured, peach cobbler is an obvious Southern invention. My version replaces the animal products with coconut oil and coconut milk, and I add a pinch of fresh ginger for a delightfully tropical cobbler.

2 pounds fresh peaches, halved, pitted, and sliced ½ inch thick, or thawed frozen sliced peaches

1 cup coconut sugar

1 teaspoon grated or minced peeled fresh ginger

1 tablespoon coconut oil

1 (14-ounce) can full-fat coconut milk

1 teaspoon apple cider vinegar

1 ½ cups unbleached all-purpose flour

2 teaspoons baking powder

¼ teaspoon salt

1. Preheat the oven to 350°F.

2. In a large saucepan combine the peaches, ½ cup of the sugar, the ginger, and 2 tablespoons water. Bring it to a simmer and cook until the peaches begin to soften, 5 to 7 minutes.

3. Place the oil in an 8 × 8-inch baking dish and set it in the oven for 5 minutes to melt.

4. In a small bowl, whisk together the coconut milk and vinegar.

5. In a medium bowl, whisk together the flour, remaining ½ cup sugar, baking powder, and salt. Pour the coconut milk mixture into the flour mixture and whisk gently to combine. Do not overmix.

6. Scrape the batter into the baking dish right over the melted coconut oil. Don't stir it. Scrape the syrupy peach filling evenly over the batter. Don't stir this either. Bake for 30 minutes until the batter is baked through and the peaches are slightly golden.

7. Let the cobbler cool for at least 15 minutes, then serve warm. Bourbon Vanilla Ice Cream (page 184) is a perfect accompaniment. Leftover peach cobbler can be stored in the refrigerator for up to 3 days.

NO-BAKE STONE FRUIT cobbler

· · · · · · ·

serves 4

Before becoming vegan, I had no idea that a healthy dessert could exist and actually taste as good as the buttery, sugary kind. Boy, was I wrong! Raw desserts made with fresh seasonal fruit, fatty nuts, sweet dates, and all the right spices are totally fulfilling and 100 percent guilt-free. I especially like making raw desserts in the summer, when I don't want to turn my oven on. This no-bake cobbler can be tossed together in minutes! Feel free to replace the stone fruit with different seasonal fruits throughout the year.

2 ripe medium peaches, halved, pitted, and sliced ¼ inch thick

1 pound cherries, pitted and halved (about 2 cups)

2 tablespoons freshly squeezed orange juice

1 ½ cups pecans

½ cup chopped pitted Medjool dates

1 teaspoon pure vanilla extract

Dash of ground cinnamon

Pinch of sea salt

1. In a large bowl, toss the peaches and cherries with the orange juice.

2. In a food processor, pulse the pecans, dates, vanilla, cinnamon, and salt until a hearty nut crumble is achieved. Scrape the crumble onto the sliced fruit, toss lightly, and spoon into a pie dish or onto dessert plates to serve.

3. This dessert will stay fresh in the refrigerator for up to 2 days.

STRAWBERRY
shortcake

● ● ● ● ● ● ●

serves **4**

This strawberry shortcake is healthy enough to eat for breakfast, and I've done so many times. I used to teach this recipe in my Vegan Basics cooking class because it demonstrates the simplicity of vegan baking and proves that it doesn't require magic skills or fancy, hard-to-find ingredients.

There are many ways to make a strawberry shortcake, and in the South it's often made with leftover piecrust. This cakey version, however, is my favorite.

SHORTCAKE

2 cups whole wheat pastry flour

2 teaspoons baking powder

¼ teaspoon baking soda

2 tablespoons cane sugar

¾ teaspoon salt

1 (14-ounce) can full-fat coconut milk

STRAWBERRY FILLING

**1 pound fresh strawberries, hulled and halved, or
    1 (16-ounce) bag frozen strawberries, thawed**

1 teaspoon freshly squeezed lemon juice

2 tablespoons cane sugar

1 teaspoon arrowroot powder or cornstarch

WHIPPED COCONUT CREAM

1½ cups coconut cream, chilled

3 tablespoons cane sugar

1½ teaspoons pure vanilla extract

1. Preheat the oven to 400°F.

2. Make the shortcake: In a large bowl, whisk together the flour, baking powder, baking soda, sugar, and salt. Stir in coconut milk. Do not overmix.

3. Scrape the batter evenly into an 8 × 8-inch baking dish. Bake for 20 minutes, until a toothpick comes out clean.

4. Make the strawberry filling: Place the strawberries in a small saucepan with the lemon juice and sugar over medium heat and bring to a simmer. Stir in the arrowroot, breaking up any clumps. Reduce the heat to low and keep stirring until the strawberries are creamy and thick. Set aside.

5. Make the whipped cream: Place the coconut cream, sugar, and vanilla in a small bowl and mix with a handheld mixer on high speed for 3 to 5 minutes, until firm peaks have formed. (Alternatively, you can whisk it vigorously by hand.)

6. Remove the shortcake from the oven and let it cool for 10 minutes. Cut it into 9 squares and then use a spatula to remove each square. Cut the squares in half and spoon the strawberry filling on the bottom half. Replace the top layer and top with a dollop of coconut cream.

7. Unassembled strawberry shortcakes can stay fresh up to 3 days. Store the cakes at room temperature, and the filling and coconut cream in the refrigerator.

CREAM CHEESE *pound* CAKE

• • • • • • •

**makes 1 9 × 5-inch loaf pan
or 1 6-cup Bundt pan**

Sweet childhood memories come flooding into my mind when I smell pound cake baking. This was the only cake I wanted on my birthday, and my nana would bake one for me every year. I was very nervous about veganizing this cake because I wanted it to be everything that I remembered from my childhood: moist, dense, and perfectly sweet. Turns out vegan cream cheese is a great replacement for the dairy version, and vinegar reacts with the baking powder and baking soda to guarantee a cake with the perfect amount of rise and body. Make this for any nonvegan, and I promise you they won't know the difference and will come back asking for more.

1 cup plain unsweetened soy milk or other nondairy milk

1 tablespoon apple cider vinegar

2 cups unbleached all-purpose flour

1 ½ teaspoons baking powder

½ teaspoon baking soda

½ teaspoon salt

½ cup vegan cream cheese

¼ cup vegan butter, at room temperature

1 cup cane sugar

2 teaspoons pure vanilla extract

1. Preheat the oven to 350°F. Grease and flour a loaf pan or line it with parchment paper and set aside.

2. In a small bowl, stir together the soy milk and vinegar and set aside to curdle for 5 minutes.

3. In a medium bowl, sift together the flour, baking powder, baking soda, and salt.

4. In the bowl of a standing mixer fitted with the whisk attachment, beat together the vegan cream cheese and butter on medium-high speed until creamy, about 2 minutes. (Alternatively, you can use a hand mixer.) Add the sugar and continue to beat for 3 minutes until it's fluffy. Add the vanilla and soy milk–vinegar mixture and beat on low until the ingredients are incorporated. Slowly add the dry ingredients until just combined. Do not overmix.

5. Scrape the batter evenly into the prepared loaf pan. Bake for 50 to 55 minutes, until a toothpick comes out clean.

6. Remove the cake from the oven and let cool for 20 minutes. Remove the loaf to a cooling rack and cool completely before serving.

7. Store leftover cake in a cake dish or airtight container for up to 3 days.

SWEET POTATO *yeast* DONUTS

• • • • • • • •

makes about 15 donuts

Shocker! Donuts were not invented in the South, but Krispy Kreme sure was, and that's enough for me. These sweet potato yeast donuts are light, fluffy, and satisfying. The sweet potato takes them to the next level. Top them with sweet potato glaze, and enjoy one with a hot cup of Louisiana chicory coffee for a truly Southern experience.

¾ cup plain unsweetened soy milk or other nondairy milk

3 tablespoons vegan butter

3 tablespoons warm water (95°F to 105°F)

1 (¼-ounce) package (2¼ teaspoons) active dry yeast

1½ cups unbleached all-purpose flour, plus more for dusting

½ teaspoon salt

½ teaspoon ground cinnamon

¾ cup mashed sweet potato (from 1 baked medium sweet potato)

3 tablespoons sugar

5 cups coconut oil, for frying

Sweet Potato Donut Glaze (recipe follows)

1. Place the soy milk and vegan butter in a small saucepan and warm it on low heat until the butter has melted. Remove from the heat and set aside.

2. Pour the water into a small bowl, then sprinkle the yeast over it to dissolve for about 5 minutes.

3. In a another small bowl, stir together the flour, salt, and cinnamon.

4. In the bowl of a standing mixer fitted with the whisk attachment, beat together the mashed sweet potato and sugar on medium-high speed until soft and fluffy. (Alternatively, you can use a hand mixer.) Pour the soy milk mixture and yeast mixture into the sweet potato and continue to beat until well combined. Using the dough attachment, slowly add the dry ingredients. (If you don't have a dough attachment, use a wooden spoon to incorporate the ingredients. Once it becomes too difficult to stir, use your hands to knead.)

5. Flour a clean work surface and transfer the dough onto the floured work space. Knead until you've got a smooth dough ball. Lightly oil a large bowl. Place the dough ball in it, cover with plastic wrap or a kitchen towel, and let it rise for 1 hour. The dough should triple in size.

recipe continues ☞

6. Line a baking sheet with parchment paper or a silicone mat and keep nearby.

7. Remove the dough from the bowl and press it down on the floured work space to release air. Use a floured rolling pin to roll the dough about ½ inch thick. Use a donut cutter to cut the dough into donut shapes, then carefully transfer them to the prepared baking sheet. Repeat the dough rolling and shape cutting with the remaining dough. Cover the baking sheet with a clean kitchen towel and set aside. Let the donuts rise for a second time, about 30 minutes.

8. In a large dutch oven or heavy-bottomed pot, heat the oil to 365°F. Double-line a cooling rack with paper towels and keep nearby.

9. Carefully drop the donuts—3 or 4 at a time—and donut holes into the oil. Do not overcrowd. Fry on each side for about 3 minutes. The donuts should turn a soft golden brown. If they brown too quickly, the oil is too hot, so you'll want to reduce the heat.

10. Use a handled sieve or slotted spoon to remove the donuts from the oil. Transfer them to the prepared cooling rack and allow them to cool for at least 20 minutes.

11. Once cool, dip 1 side of each donut into the sweet potato glaze, then set them glazed side up on a cooling rack for the glaze to harden, about 5 minutes, before eating.

12. Donuts are best eaten the day they are made.

SWEET POTATO DONUT GLAZE

• • • • • • •

makes ½ cup

¼ cup mashed sweet potato (from ¼ baked medium sweet potato)

1 cup confectioners' sugar

2 tablespoons plain unsweetened soy milk or other nondairy milk

Place the sweet potato, sugar, and soy milk in a food processor and blend until creamy and smooth. Transfer it to small shallow bowl and use to glaze the donuts.

SWEET POTATO— *tahini* COOKIES

• • • • • • • •

makes **12 to 16 cookies**

This is one of my favorite cookie recipes! It's my take on the oatmeal cookie and replaces butter with nutritious tahini—sesame seed paste. Tahini is high in vitamin E, calcium, and copper, making it great for your hair, skin, and bones.

The sweet potato and pecans help round out the healthfulness of these delicious cookies. You may have a hard time getting them into the oven because the batter is amazing!

NOTE: To shred a sweet potato, peel at least ½ medium sweet potato and use a handheld or box grater to shred about ¼ cup. That is about ¼ medium sweet potato. Save the leftover sweet potato to use in another recipe.

1 cup tahini

½ cup pure maple syrup

1 teaspoon pure vanilla extract

1 teaspoon ground cinnamon

¼ cup shredded peeled sweet potato (see Note)

3 tablespoons dark chocolate chips

1 ½ cups quick-cooking oats

¾ cup chopped pecans

Pinch of sea salt

1. Preheat the oven to 350°F. Line a cookie sheet with parchment paper or a silicone mat and set aside.

2. In a medium bowl, use a fork to stir together the tahini, maple syrup, vanilla, cinnamon, and sweet potato. Add the chocolate chips, oats, pecans, and salt and stir well to combine. The batter will be sticky.

3. Dampen your hands and scoop 2 or 3 tablespoons into your palm to form a flattened cookie shape. Place the cookie on the prepared baking sheet and repeat with the remaining batter. Bake cookies for 10 to 12 minutes, or until they're slightly browned on the bottom.

4. Remove from the oven and let the cookies cool on a rack for 10 minutes before enjoying.

SWEET POTATO *sugar* COOKIES

• • • • • • • •

makes 16 cookies

Fancy up your Christmas cookie tray with these buttery sugar cookies made with mashed sweet potato. These cookies are fun to make and decorate with kids.

These sweet potato sugar cookies are best made with a hand mixer or standing mixer, but if you have neither, a bit of elbow grease will get the job done. Store the cookies in an airtight container at room temperature for up to 1 week.

½ cup vegan butter

¼ cup cane sugar, plus more for topping

¼ cup brown sugar or coconut sugar

3 tablespoons mashed sweet potato (from 1 baked small sweet potato; reserve leftovers for another use)

1 teaspoon pure vanilla extract

1 ¼ cups spelt flour or unbleached all-purpose flour, plus more for dusting

1 teaspoon baking powder

¼ teaspoon salt

OPTIONAL ICING

½ cup confectioners' sugar

1 to 2 teaspoons plain unsweetened soy milk, or other nondairy milk

1. In the bowl of a standing mixer fitted with the whisk attachment, beat together the vegan butter and sugars on high speed until fluffy, about 2 minutes. (Alternatively, you can use a hand mixer.) Add the mashed sweet potato and vanilla and continue to beat until creamy. Replace the whisk attachment with the flat beater attachment, then add the flour, baking powder, and salt slowly and beat until well combined.

2. Gently gather the dough into a ball, then flatten it into a 1-inch-thick disk and cover with plastic wrap. Place it in the refrigerator to firm for about 30 minutes.

3. Preheat the oven to 350°F. Line 2 baking sheets with parchment paper.

4. Lightly flour a clean work surface and transfer the dough onto the work space. Use a floured rolling pin to roll out the dough about ⅛ inch thick. Use a cookie cutter to cut out shapes and gently place them on the baking sheets. Repeat the rolling and cutting with the scraps. Top the cookies with a sprinkle of cane sugar and bake for 10 minutes, or until slightly golden on the bottom.

5. Remove from the oven and let them cool on a rack for 10 minutes. For a quick icing, whisk together the confectioners' sugar with the soy milk to form a paste, then transfer to a piping bag to use.

CARAMELIZED *coconut* GRILLED PEACHES

● ● ● ● ● ● ● ●

serves **4**

This is the ultimate grown-up summer dessert. Grilling the peaches caramelizes their sugars, creating a complex pairing if you choose to serve them with Bourbon Vanilla Ice Cream (page 184). Make this dessert when you want to treat yourself to something fancy or when you've got company. It's an easy dessert to put together, but your guests will be so impressed. If you don't have a grill, you can place the prepared peaches under the broiler for 5 minutes.

1 tablespoon coconut oil

2 ripe large peaches, halved and pitted

2 tablespoons coconut sugar or brown sugar

½ teaspoon ground cinnamon

4 scoops of Bourbon Vanilla Ice Cream (page 184)

½ cup chopped toasted pecans (see Note on page 164)

1. Preheat a clean indoor or outdoor grill to medium heat.

2. Rub a bit of the coconut oil on the cut side of each peach, then sprinkle ½ tablespoon of the coconut sugar on each peach half, followed by a pinch of cinnamon.

3. Place the peaches cut-side down onto the grill and cook for 5 minutes, or until grill marks are visible and the sugars caramelize.

4. Remove from the grill and let the peaches cool for 5 minutes before serving. They're delicious as is, but you can also top them with Bourbon Vanilla Ice Cream and toasted pecans.

BOURBON
vanilla
ICE CREAM

· · · · · · ·

makes 1 pint

Creamy homemade ice cream is one of my favorite things to make during the warmer months. I've actually come to prefer it over the many brands you can buy at the grocery store. I love to play around with different flavor combinations. This is one of my favorites: simple boozy bourbon and smooth vanilla.

2 cups full-fat coconut cream or full-fat coconut milk

¾ cup cane sugar

1 tablespoon light corn syrup

¼ teaspoon sea salt

1 teaspoon pure vanilla extract

1 tablespoon bourbon

1. In a medium saucepan, stir together the coconut cream, sugar, corn syrup, and salt over medium heat until the liquid temperature reaches 160°F (or just starts to simmer). Continue stirring until the sugar dissolves.

2. Remove from the heat and stir in the vanilla and bourbon. Allow it to cool completely, then pour it into a container to chill in the refrigerator for at least 6 hours.

3. When the cream is chilled, churn the ice cream according to your ice cream maker's instructions.

4. Scrape the churned ice cream into a wide pint-size freezer-safe container and let the ice cream freeze and solidify for at least 2 hours before serving. Enjoy on its own or serve on top of the Caramelized Coconut Grilled Peaches (page 182).

COCONUT-PECAN *pralines*

• • • • • • • •

makes 2 dozen candies

When French settlers landed in Louisiana, they brought along pralines, a candy nougat made with almonds and sugar. Of course, down south they were transformed with pecans. Traditional Louisiana pralines are made with pecans, cream, butter, and lots of sugar. For this vegan version, I replaced the cream and butter with a coconut-based vegan alternative. It works just as well and gives the pralines a pleasant coconut flavor.

Humidity is the enemy of pralines, so keep that in mind when preparing these during the warmer months. On humid days, try making them in an air-conditioned kitchen.

1 cup granulated sugar

1 cup brown sugar

½ cup coconut cream

2 tablespoons vegan butter

1 teaspoon pure vanilla extract

1 cup roughly chopped lightly toasted pecans (see Note on page 164)

1. Line a baking sheet with waxed or parchment paper and set aside.

2. Place the sugars and coconut cream in a small saucepan over medium heat. Stir with a wooden spoon to help the sugars dissolve while you bring the mixture to a full boil. Use a candy thermometer to bring the boiling mixture to 235°F to 240°F. If you don't have a thermometer, boiling it for about 3 minutes should get you there.

3. Remove from the heat and stir in the vegan butter, vanilla, and toasted pecans. Continue to stir until the mixture begins to thicken, about 2 minutes.

4. Drop heaping tablespoon-size dollops of the mixture onto the prepared baking sheet. Let the pralines cool completely and harden for at least 1 hour before enjoying.

5. Store the pralines in an airtight container at room temperature for up to 2 weeks.

PLUM *verbena* SORBET

• • • • • • •

makes 1 pint

This refreshing treat has become one of my favorite summer desserts. My family has always loved plums, but we never used them in recipes. Turns out plums make an incredible and creamy sorbet. For this recipe I always use Italian prune plums, which I find at my local farmers' market. They're reliably sweet, have a strong plum flavor, and the pit in the middle pops out easily. If you cannot find them, substitute another plum. They should be ripe but not overripe. Fragrant lemon verbena, which you can also find at the farmers' market (or grow it at home), adds more dimension and lemony flavor to this sorbet. But if you can't get your hands on it, use fresh basil, lemon basil, or mint.

1 cup sugar

2 pounds ripe plums, halved, pitted, then quartered

6 fresh lemon verbena leaves

2 tablespoons light corn syrup

1 teaspoon lemon juice

1. Place the sugar and ½ cup water in a large saucepan over high heat. Once it begins to simmer, reduce the heat to medium-low and add the plums and verbena leaves. Continue to simmer until the plums begin to soften, about 8 minutes. Stir in the corn syrup and lemon juice, then remove from the heat and let the plum mixture cool for about 15 minutes. Pour the cooled mixture into a blender and blend until silky smooth.

2. Pour the sorbet base into a 6-cup container or jar and set in the refrigerator to chill for at least 6 hours.

3. Once cool, remove the verbena leaves from the sorbet base and churn the sorbet according to your ice cream maker's instructions.

4. Scrape the churned sorbet into a wide pint-size freezer-safe container and freeze for 8 hours before serving.

no-bake SWEET POTATO GINGERBREAD BARS

· · · · · · ·

serves 8

This unique dessert is healthy and absolutely delicious—and highlights the amazing versatility of sweet potatoes! Though gingerbread has its roots in Europe, gingerroot is native to South Asia. Over the centuries, gingerbread has made its way into cultures all around the world. Ever think you'd try a no-bake version?

GINGERBREAD CRUST

1 cup almonds

1 ½ cups pitted Medjool dates

½ cup shredded unsweetened coconut

3 teaspoons molasses

1 (1 ½-inch) knob fresh ginger, peeled and minced

1 teaspoon ground cinnamon

¼ teaspoon freshly grated nutmeg

¼ teaspoon ground cloves

¼ teaspoon cayenne pepper

Pinch of sea salt

Pinch of freshly ground black pepper

1 tablespoon coconut oil

SWEET POTATO FILLING

1 ½ cups mashed sweet potato (from 1 ½ baked medium sweet potatoes)

⅓ cup pure maple syrup or coconut nectar, plus more to taste

¼ cup melted coconut oil

1 teaspoon freshly squeezed lemon juice

1 teaspoon pure vanilla extract

¼ teaspoon salt

1 ½ teaspoons ground cinnamon

¾ teaspoon ground cardamom

¾ teaspoon ground ginger

¼ teaspoon ground cloves

⅛ teaspoon freshly ground black pepper

2 tablespoons coconut flour

1. Line an 8 × 8-inch baking pan with parchment paper and set aside.

2. Make the crust: Place all the crust ingredients in a food processor and blend until well combined. Remove the lid and gather some of the crust into your hand, squeezing it to form a tight ball in your palm. If the crust crumbles and doesn't stick, you'll need to blend it some more or add another date.

3. Scrape the crumble into the prepared baking pan and press it firmly into the bottom to create a tight crust. Set aside and clean the food processor.

4. Make the filling: Place all the ingredients in the clean food processor and blend until smooth. Taste and add more maple syrup if necessary. Spoon the filling into the crust and smooth it down with the back of a large spoon or rubber spatula.

5. You can eat it right away, but I recommend letting it firm up and set. Place it in the refrigerator for at least 1 hour or up to overnight.

6. Pull the parchment paper out of the pan and cut into squares. Store gingerbread squares in an airtight container in the refrigerator for up to 1 week.

TURMERIC *& ginger* LEMONADE

● ● ● ● ● ● ●

makes 2 liters

I think about my mom when I drink lemonade. She doesn't like to cook, but she'd make the most delicious and refreshing lemonade in the hot Georgia summer. This recipe endeavors to balance out the unhealthy sugar with anti-inflammatory ginger and turmeric. Bear in mind there's still a lot of sugar in this lemonade, but it sure is terrific.

1 cup raw cane sugar

8 freshly squeezed lemons (about 1½ cups lemon juice)

1 (3-inch) knob fresh turmeric, juiced, or 1 tablespoon ground turmeric

1 (3-inch) knob peeled fresh ginger, juiced, or 2 tablespoons grated peeled fresh ginger

8 cups ice-cold water

Ice

1. In a small saucepan, bring 1 cup water to a boil, add the sugar, and stir until dissolved. Remove from the heat and let the sugar water cool.

2. In a tall 2-liter pitcher, mix the lemon juice, turmeric, and ginger. Add the cooled simple syrup and the ice-cold water and stir well. Serve over ice. Store in the refrigerator for up to 5 days.

SUMMER *molasses* ICED TEA

• • • • • • •

makes 1.5 liters

No Southern summer cookout is complete without an ice-cold pitcher of sweet tea. I love to add a couple tablespoons of blackstrap molasses to give this Southern fixture an earthier and more grown-up appeal. To make iced tea all you need is an inexpensive black tea. My family always used Lipton or Luzianne brand. The baking soda in the recipe prevents the tannins from making the tea overly bitter, so don't skip that.

6 black tea bags

⅛ teaspoon baking soda

2 cups boiling water

½ cup plus 2 tablespoons raw cane sugar (use less if you don't like it Southern sweet)

2 tablespoons blackstrap molasses

6 cups ice-cold water

Ice

1. Place the tea bags and baking soda in a large heat-safe pitcher or container. Pour the boiling water over the tea bags and steep for 15 minutes.

2. Remove the tea bags (don't squeeze them) and discard. Add the sugar and molasses and stir with a wooden spoon until they have dissolved. Add the ice-cold water and stir again. Serve over ice.

PEACH *ginger* GREEN TEA

• • • • • • •

makes 1.5 liters

Before Southerners got their hands on black tea, they were icing green tea. If you aren't in the mood for supersweet iced tea or lemonade, you'll love this unsweetened refreshment. Of course, if you love sweet tea, feel free to add sugar or sorghum syrup when the green tea is still hot. Quick tip for grating ginger: Keep a knob of peeled ginger in the freezer and wrapped in aluminum foil. Frozen ginger is extremely easy to grate into recipes.

6 green tea bags

⅛ teaspoon baking soda

1 tablespoon grated peeled fresh ginger

2 cups boiling water

6 cups ice-cold water

2 to 3 ripe medium peaches, halved, pitted, and chopped (about 2 cups)

Ice

1. Place the tea bags, baking soda, and ginger in a half gallon heat-safe pitcher or container. Pour the boiling water over the tea bags and steep for 15 minutes.

2. Remove the tea bags (don't squeeze them) and discard. Add the ice-cold water and stir in the chopped fresh peaches. Serve over ice. Store in the refrigerator for up to 5 days.

BLACKBERRY SIMPLE SYRUP & soda

· · · · · · · ·

makes 1½ cups syrup and 6 drinks

Of all the fruits you can make into a bright and tasty syrup, blackberry is my favorite. This simple syrup can be used for everything from blackberry soda to topping waffles to Blackberry Mint Juleps (page 196). You could even stir some into a glass of Peach Ginger Green Tea (page 193) or Late-Summer Sangria (page 200). Look for the freshest blackberries at your local farmers' market at the peak of their season—between July and August.

The leftover blackberry pulp can be mixed into batters or used to top pancakes, waffles, Creamy Teff Porridge (page 62), or oatmeal.

BLACKBERRY SIMPLE SYRUP

2½ cups fresh blackberries

½ cup raw cane sugar

½ teaspoon grated peeled fresh ginger (optional)

SODA

Ice

1 cup sparkling mineral water or seltzer water

¼ cup Blackberry Simple Syrup

1. Make the simple syrup: Place the blackberries and sugar in a medium saucepan. Stir well, then give the berries about 5 minutes to start releasing their juices.

2. Add ¼ cup water to the pan and place it over medium heat. If you are using ginger, add it now. Bring the berries to a simmer and cook until they have softened and fallen apart, about 15 minutes.

3. Remove the pot from the heat and let cool for 5 minutes. Strain the blackberry syrup through a fine-mesh sieve into a 16-ounce glass jar with a tight-fitting lid. Syrup will keep for at least 1 week. Reserve the pulp in another small jar to use later or discard.

⤜ TO MAKE BLACKBERRY SODA ⤛

Fill a tall glass with ice and pour in the sparkling water. Add the blackberry syrup and stir. Taste and add more syrup if desired.

BLACKBERRY *mint* JULEP

• • • • • • • •

makes 2 cocktails

This classic Kentucky Derby cocktail takes on a very Southern spin: Blackberry Simple Syrup (page 195). This is the drink you'll want to reach for on a hot summer day when you need something cold and absolutely refreshing. To make it, you will need a nut-milk bag with which to crush the ice and mint leaves.

15 fresh mint leaves

2 cups ice cubes

2 to 4 ounces Blackberry Simple Syrup (page 195)

4 ounces bourbon

Splash of plain seltzer water (optional)

1. Place the mint leaves in a nut-milk bag with the ice. Use a rolling pin or another sturdy object to crush the ice in the bag.

2. Divide the crushed mint ice between 2 highball glasses. Top each with 1 to 2 ounces of the simple syrup and 2 ounces of the bourbon. Top off with a splash of seltzer if desired.

SPICY
watermelon
MARGARITA

• • • • • • • •

makes 2 cocktails

Jalapeño pepper gives this perfectly sweet summer cocktail a nice kick. I'll often make this if I get a watermelon that tastes great but doesn't have the perfect texture. Use a very sweet watermelon to avoid having to add simple syrup. I also recommend enjoying this drink without alcohol for a healthy and hydrating refreshment.

2 cups watermelon chunks
¼ cup sugar, for the rim
1 quartered lime, for garnish
Ice
Juice of 1 lime, plus more to taste
4 thin slices of jalapeño pepper, seeded
4 ounces tequila or mezcal
1 to 1½ cups plain seltzer water

1. Place the watermelon in a blender and liquefy it. Strain the watermelon juice through a fine-mesh sieve into a 16-ounce jar. (Save the pulp by spooning it into an ice cube tray and freezing it for watermelon ice cubes.)

2. Place sugar in a medium-size bowl. Rub 1 cut lime wedge along the rim of the serving glasses, then dip into the sugar to coat the rim. Fill 2 8-ounce glasses with ice, pour ¾ cup watermelon juice into each glass, and divide the lime juice between the glasses. Drop 2 slices of jalapeño into each glass, then top each with 2 ounces of the tequila and ½ to ¾ cup of seltzer water. Give them a stir, garnish with more lime, and enjoy.

LATE-SUMMER
SANGRIA, page 200

PEACH COLADA,
page 201

SPICY WATERMELON
MARGARITA, page 197

LATE-SUMMER
sangria

• • • • • • • •

makes 2 liters

White wine and rosé are great summer drinks, but given the option, I'll always choose a fruity homemade sangria. A dry Pinot Grigio and aged bourbon work best in this Southern cocktail, as do very ripe fresh peaches and berries. For the best sangria, make this a few hours before serving so that the fruit has plenty of time to impart its flavor.

¼ cup sugar

2 ripe medium peaches, halved, pitted, and chopped (about 1½ cups)

1 cup blackberries

1 cup sliced hulled strawberries

1 750 ml bottle very cold Pinot Grigio

5 ounces bourbon

1. Make the simple syrup: Dissolve the sugar in ¼ cup boiling water. Let it cool completely before adding to the sangria.

2. Place the peaches and berries in a 2-liter pitcher. Add the wine, bourbon, and simple syrup. Stir well. Refrigerate the sangria for at least 1 hour before serving.

PEACH
colada

• • • • • • •

makes 2 cocktails

Peach, pineapple, and coconut are a match made in heaven, and this cocktail will take you there. Most piña colada recipes call for sweetened cream of coconut, but we'll skip the cane sugar and use the thick cream from the top of a can of coconut cream and pineapple juice to get that tropical flavor. This cocktail can also be made alcohol-free.

2 cups ice cubes

4 ounces rum

¼ cup unsweetened coconut cream

¼ cup full-fat coconut milk

¼ cup pineapple juice

¼ cup fresh or frozen peach chunks

2 peach or pineapple slices, for garnish

Place all the ingredients in a blender and blend until creamy yet still frozen. Divide between 2 tall glasses and garnish each with a peach slice.

PANTRY STAPLES & SAUCES

· · · · · · · · · · · · · · · · · · ·

THE WORD *SAUCE* **COMES FROM THE** Latin *sal*, which means "to salt." This of course means to elevate the flavor, draw out flavors from the food, and make a meal complete. Whether it's creamy, tangy, spicy, or sweet, a delicious sauce is exactly what you need to add pizzazz to any dish.

The sauces in this chapter show up in recipes throughout this book, but I encourage you to find new exciting ways to use them in your daily cooking. Having a variety of tasty sauces in your refrigerator at all times makes it so much easier to dress up otherwise plain meals. Dollop some Pecan Muhammara (page 214) on a boring bowl of rice and broccoli and all of a sudden you've got a crazy-delicious creation. Have a dry meal that could use a bit of moisture? Add some Spicy Peach-Tomatillo Salsa (page 212) or Ooooh Mama Mushroom Gravy (page 205). If you're meal prepping for the week, make sure to make at least two different sauces to dress things up. Where I'm from, the premier sauce is, of course, barbecue, and Bourbon BBQ Sauce (page 208) won't disappoint.

ooooh mama MUSHROOM GRAVY

• • • • • • • •

makes 2 cups

Use this savory gravy to raise the delicious dial on Lentil Loaf (page 138), mashed potatoes, biscuits, or plain ol' boiled rice (one of my childhood simple delights). It makes use of a very special ingredient, porcini powder—dried porcini mushrooms ground into a soft powder that can be used to add that rich mushroom meaty umami-ness to whatever you're making. It's a pricey specialty item, so it's not required to make this delicious gravy, but if you're willing to spend some cash (about $20 for a large container that will last you at least one year), look for it online. Porcini powder is an especially fantastic ingredient to keep around if you are cooking for meat lovers who are often craving umami flavors.

1 tablespoon grapeseed oil

10 ounces baby bella mushrooms, thinly sliced (about 2 cups)

Salt

2 tablespoons unbleached all-purpose flour

2 cups Veggie Mineral Stock (page 88) or 2 cups water plus 1 teaspoon vegetable bouillon paste

2 teaspoons porcini powder (optional)

1 teaspoon freshly ground black pepper

1 teaspoon dried rosemary

1 tablespoon nutritional yeast

½ tablespoon tamari soy sauce

1. In a large saucepan, heat the oil over medium heat. Add the mushrooms and a pinch of salt and sauté until they are tender, about 7 minutes.

2. Add the flour and stir well. Let the flour toast for about 30 seconds. Then add the stock, porcini powder, if using, pepper, and rosemary and stir. Bring to a simmer and reduce the heat to medium-low. Continue to cook and reduce the gravy for 30 minutes until it thickens.

3. Stir in the nutritional yeast and tamari and season to taste with salt. Remove from the heat and let the gravy cool for 10 minutes before serving.

FINGER-LICKIN' BARBECUE SAUCE

Barbecue sauce was most certainly conceived for use on meat of all kinds, but today vegans use it to give all sorts of vegetables rich, succulent appeal. The first commercial barbecue sauce is said to have been from Atlanta, Georgia, just like me. I take that as a sign that my love for this sweet and tangy sauce was fated.

Barbecue sauce is made differently throughout the South, but most sauces share a few common ingredients: vinegar, Worcestershire sauce, ketchup, and usually mustard. Vinegar has long been used to baste meats and, along with the other three, to balance smoked food. The combination of tangy vinegar, sweet ketchup, salty Worcestershire sauce, and spicy mustard makes the perfect condiment to liven up any grilled food, vegetables included.

Growing up we always bought barbecue sauce at the grocery store, but from the moment I first tasted homemade barbecue sauce, I have never looked back. First off, homemade sauce is supereasy to make. Second, store-bought sauce has been pasteurized and simply cannot compete with the bright and fresh flavor of barbecue sauce made at home with love. Third, the combinations are endless! My favorite sauces utilize fresh Southern produce, like peaches, bourbon, or other unique additions.

PEACH-DATE *bbq* SAUCE

• • • • • • • •

makes 2 cups

1 tablespoon grapeseed or canola oil

1 cup chopped Vidalia onion

2 garlic cloves, minced

1 tablespoon minced or grated peeled fresh ginger

4 ripe medium peaches, pitted and chopped (about 3 to 4 cups)

4 large Medjool dates, pitted and chopped

¼ cup ketchup

2 tablespoons soy sauce

1 ½ tablespoons Dijon mustard

1 ½ tablespoons molasses

2 teaspoons vegan Worcestershire sauce

2 teaspoons liquid smoke

2 teaspoons apple cider vinegar

2 teaspoons smoked paprika

This summery barbecue sauce uses fresh peaches (preferably from Georgia) and rich Medjool dates to replace the cane sugar. The results are nothing less than finger-lickin' good! For best results, use fresh ripe peaches, though if you get an itching for this sauce in the dead of winter, feel free to use frozen peaches. This sauce can be used on Jackfruit Sliders (page 135) or with any vegetables, tofu, tempeh, or mushrooms.

1. In a medium saucepan, heat the oil over medium heat. Add the onion, garlic, and ginger and sauté until the onion is translucent, about 3 minutes.

2. Stir in the chopped peaches and cook until they begin to soften and release their liquid, about 3 minutes. Add the dates, ketchup, soy sauce, mustard, molasses, vegan Worcestershire sauce, liquid smoke, vinegar, and paprika and stir well to combine. Bring to a low simmer over medium-low heat, partially cover the pan with a lid, and cook for 15 minutes.

3. Using a handheld immersion blender, blend the mixture until it becomes a thick sauce. To use a standing blender, allow the mixture to cool at least 15 minutes before blending. Use the sauce immediately or store it in a tightly sealed glass jar in the refrigerator for up to 1 week.

BOURBON
bbq
SAUCE

• • • • • • •

makes 2 cups

1 tablespoon grapeseed or canola oil

1 cup chopped Vidalia or yellow onion

2 garlic cloves, minced

⅓ cup bourbon

¼ cup ketchup

¼ cup tomato paste

2 tablespoons soy sauce

1 ½ tablespoons molasses

1 ½ tablespoons Dijon mustard

1 tablespoon vegan Worcestershire sauce

1 tablespoon liquid smoke

2 teaspoons apple cider vinegar

Bourbon has got to be the best liquor to cook with. It's sweet and bold and pairs well with recipes both sweet and savory. Don't go spending a whole bunch of money on a fancy bottle of bourbon to use for cooking. A well-aged inexpensive bottle, like Fighting Cock, will do the trick in this recipe and the others in this book, including cocktails.

1. In a medium saucepan, heat the oil over medium heat. Add the onion and garlic and sauté until the onion is translucent, about 3 minutes.

2. Add the bourbon and let it simmer for about 10 seconds. Then add the ketchup, tomato paste, soy sauce, molasses, mustard, vegan Worcestershire sauce, liquid smoke, and vinegar and stir well to combine. Reduce the heat to medium-low, cover the pot, and let it gently simmer for 20 minutes. The sauce should look thick, and the vegetables should be very soft.

3. Using an immersion blender (or standing blender), blend the mixture until it becomes a thick sauce. Use immediately or store the sauce in a tightly sealed glass jar in the refrigerator for up to 1 week.

RED PEPPER *aioli*

- - - - - - -

makes 2 cups

This simple aioli is easy to make and adds the perfect amount of creaminess and tang to almost any dish. I especially recommend using it for the Happy Hearts "Crab" Cakes (page 129) and the Sweet Potato Burgers (page 156).

½ cup vegan mayonnaise

1 red large bell pepper, roasted (see Note on page 214)

¼ cup chopped fresh dill

1 tablespoon red wine vinegar

1 teaspoon cane sugar (optional)

1 teaspoon freshly ground black pepper

Place all the ingredients in a blender and blend until creamy.

FIGGIN' *peachy* JAM

• • • • • • •

makes about 3 cups

When summer starts to come to an end, I can't help but want to take a souvenir with me into the cooler months. This fig and peach jam is the perfect reminder of lazy summer days, bees buzzing, and the sweet smell of ripening fruit. Feel free to sterilize your canning jar.

1 pound (2 to 3) ripe peaches, halved, pitted, and chopped
1 pound (1 pint) fresh figs, quartered
1 cup raw cane sugar
1 teaspoon freshly squeezed lemon juice

1. Place the peaches and figs in a medium pot over medium heat. Cover with the sugar, stir well, and bring to a simmer. Reduce the heat to medium-low and continue to cook until the fruit has softened, about 15 minutes. Remove from the heat and stir in the lemon juice.

2. Let the jam cool completely. Store the jam in tightly sealed glass jars in the refrigerator for up to 7 days or in the freezer for up to 3 months.

GEORGIA-PEACH *vinaigrette*

● ● ● ● ● ● ●

makes about 1½ cups

I love a fruity vinaigrette. The marriage of sweet, tangy, and salty helps bring life to simple salads and grains. I also love using this dressing on grilled vegetables. Make sure you use the best peaches you can get your hands on. They should be perfectly ripe, not overripe. When peaches aren't available, use strawberries, fresh figs, or ripe pears in their place.

2 ripe medium peaches, halved, pitted, and chopped (1½ to 2 cups)

2 tablespoons apple cider vinegar

2 tablespoons Dijon mustard

1 teaspoon dried thyme

1½ teaspoons sea salt

1 teaspoon freshly ground black pepper

¼ cup extra-virgin olive oil

1. Place the peaches, vinegar, mustard, thyme, salt, and pepper in a blender and blend until well combined. Slowly drizzle in the oil and continue to blend until creamy.

2. Use immediately or store the vinaigrette in a tightly sealed glass jar for up to 1 week.

spicy PEACH-TOMATILLO SALSA

• • • • • • • •

makes 1 cup

Peaches make everything better, especially salsa. This roasted tomatillo salsa was inspired by the spicy green salsa at my favorite Mexican restaurant in Georgia. It is a necessity on the Cajun Blackened Tofu Sandwich (page 151) and can also be served with fresh tortilla chips, on tacos, and over beans and rice.

1 pound tomatillos, husked and rinsed

1 jalapeño pepper

2 ripe medium peaches, halved, pitted, and chopped (about 1 cup)

¼ cup chopped fresh cilantro

¼ cup chopped red onion

1 teaspoon salt

1. Place a rack in the top of the oven and a second rack in the middle of the oven. Preheat the broiler.

2. Place the tomatillos and jalapeño on a baking sheet. Place the chopped peaches in another smaller oven-safe baking dish.

3. Place the tomatillos and jalapeño on the oven's top rack and broil until they begin to char and soften, about 15 minutes. Flip the tomatillos and jalapeño to char the other side for about 10 minutes. Roast the peaches on your oven's lower rack for 15 minutes.

4. Place the roasted tomatillos, jalapeño, and peaches in a blender and add the cilantro, onion, and salt. Pulse a few times to combine. Do not overblend. The salsa should be slightly chunky. Let the salsa cool before serving.

5. Store the salsa in a tightly sealed glass jar in the refrigerator for up to 5 days.

CIDER CRANBERRY *sauce*

• • • • • • •

makes 2 cups

Cranberry sauce isn't a Southern thing, but I just couldn't help but include this soulful recipe that'll be perfect for Thanksgiving and Christmas. Serve this with a hefty helping of Lentil Loaf (page 138) for the perfect combination.

12 ounces fresh or frozen cranberries

½ cup plus 2 tablespoons coconut sugar or granulated sugar

½ cup apple cider

1 teaspoon pure vanilla extract

1. In a medium saucepan over medium heat, stir together the cranberries and sugar. Pour in the cider and bring the contents to a simmer. Stir in the vanilla, then reduce the heat to low, continuing to simmer until the cranberries begin to soften and break apart, about 15 minutes.

2. Remove from the heat and let the sauce cool and thicken for about 10 minutes. Transfer the sauce to a medium bowl to cool for another 30 minutes. The sauce will continue to thicken as it cools. Serve at room temperature. Store in the refrigerator for up to 7 days.

PECAN MUHAMMARA

• • • • • • • •

makes 1½ to 2 cups

1 cup chopped lightly toasted pecans (see Note on page 164)

1 large red bell pepper, roasted (see Note)

1 small garlic clove, chopped

1 tablespoon freshly squeezed lemon juice

1 tablespoon pomegranate molasses

1 tablespoon ground Aleppo pepper

1 teaspoon ground cumin

¼ cup unseasoned bread crumbs

1 tablespoon olive oil

I remember my first taste of *muhammara.* It was at my aunt Cathy's house in New York City. I had just moved to the city, and her love of cooking and *muhammara* made me feel at home. Traditionally, this Syrian red pepper dip is made with walnuts, but I brought it down home with the addition of Georgia pecans. *Muhammara* is made with one very special ingredient, Aleppo pepper. Look for it online or at your local Middle Eastern market. If you can't find it, substitute 1 teaspoon sweet smoked paprika plus a dash of cayenne pepper. I like to make *muhammara* by hand with a mortar and pestle, but a food processor will do the job as well. The texture should be slightly chunky, not creamy and smooth like hummus.

NOTE Homemade roasted red bell peppers are preferred for this recipe. To safely roast, place a large bell pepper on a baking sheet under the broiler for 10 to 20 minutes, flipping halfway through. The skins should char and the flesh will become tender. Let the pepper cool before removing the skins.

1. Place the pecans, roasted bell pepper, garlic, lemon juice, molasses, Aleppo pepper, and cumin in a food processor. Pulse until the ingredients are well combined and still slightly chunky. (Alternatively, you can work the ingredients in a mortar using the pestle.) Pour in the bread crumbs and oil and blend until combined.

2. Serve over Smoky Black-eyed Pea Cakes (page 154), Sweet Potato Burgers (page 156), or as a dip for vegetables. It will stay fresh in the refrigerator for up to 5 days.

ACKNOWLEDGMENTS

. . . .

WRITING THIS COOKBOOK WAS A dream come true. I am filled with love and gratitude for the people, animals, and spirits that supported and guided me through this journey.

To my ancestors who created soul food and against all odds laid the foundation for my interpretation of this American tradition. "I am my ancestors' wildest dreams." —Unknown.

To my partner, Maxx: I can never thank you enough for your boundless support, patience, love, and words of wisdom. You are an incredible editor, recipe-tester, accidental personal assistant, and best friend. I'm so grateful for the love, positivity, and peace you bring to our life together. *Sweet Potato Soul* wouldn't be awesome without you.

To my magical nana: The support and love you've given me every day of my life has made me the person I am today. I live in the kitchen because of you. I love food because of you. I know compassion because of you. And I follow my dreams because of you. You make me laugh and inspire me at the same time. Despite the physical distance between us, you are always in my heart. This book is for you, Nana!!

To my parents: Mommy, I think your disgust at the red meat section in grocery stores and love for animals destined me to become vegan, which has been life-changing in so many wonderful ways. Thank you for challenging me to dream big and supporting me through all of my phases: aspiring dancer, actress, designer, psychologist . . . You've taught me the value of hard work, how to be healthy, and to always believe in myself. For all these things, I am eternally grateful.

Daddy, you're the one who introduced me to a vegan lifestyle. I remember you telling me about your days working at SoulVeg in Atlanta and experimenting with a raw food lifestyle in Chicago. You're an OG vegan chef!! Do you know how cool that makes you? Thank you, too, for inspiring me, supporting my many aspirations, and challenging me to be great.

To Aunt Anna: Your passion for creativity and art has made such a big impact in my life,

and so has your vegetarianism. You've shaped me in more ways than you know. Thank you for always loving and praying for me.

To Cathy Loup: One of the biggest perks of being with Maxx is getting you as my auntie. I've learned so much about food and cooking from you, and you inspire me with every meal you serve us. Thank you for being so supportive of my journey from actress to personal chef to *Sweet Potato Soul*. And I thank you for your support at every stage of this book writing process: from editor to recipe-tester.

To my living grandparents: For each of you I have a food memory that I keep close to my heart. Nana: baked sweet potatoes, my favorite simple delight. You'd always tell me about your aunt Mamie, who liked to eat leftover sweet potatoes cold right out of the fridge . . . I do that, too. Larry and Kathy: I'd never even heard of pumpkin pie until we came to your house one year for Thanksgiving. Did I eat the whole thing? Milton: Huge jars of garlic in the refrigerator. That's what I call healthy!

To Grandma Sandra: I remember you reading your book *Cuckoo Head* to me and the pride you had for the children's book that you published. I still feel that pride for you, and my first published book is in your memory.

To Diane Loup: You're the best mother-in-love that a girl could have. Thank you for supporting Maxx and me on our vegan journey, for cooking for us, and for always being so curious and open-minded. Thank you for supporting my creative and business endeavors and experiments, and always sharing my wins.

To Eric Yu, Peter Lu, and my Peacefood family: Working at Peacefood Café was the best job ever. Thank you, Eric and Peter, for showing us how to run an ethical and conscious business. It was at Peacefood that I learned about ethical veganism and about our power to change the world by doing good. My Peacefood friends were my first blog readers, YouTube subscribers, and client referrals. I am forever grateful for my time spent working with you.

To my mentors Bryant Terry and Latham Thomas: Even if you didn't know it, you both have been tremendous mentors to me since I began this journey in 2011. The integrity, excellence, and creativity of your work is immensely inspiring to me and so many other young black vegans.

To photographer extraordinaire Sidney Bensimon: We've been waxing poetic about creating a cookbook together for so many years, and finally the book is here! Thank you for your enthusiasm for my work and support as I've grown *Sweet Potato Soul*. I'm grateful to be able to make beautiful work with my friend, for everything we've done in the past, and for everything to come in the future.

To Victoria Moran: I have you to thank for getting the ball rolling on this cookbook. I didn't even realize I could get a book deal until that day on the 3 train. Thank you for believing in me and for introducing me to Steve Troha. You are an inspiration to me, and I feel so honored to call you my friend.

To Donna Loffredo, my editor: I could tell we'd work well together the first time we talked on the phone. It has been an absolute pleasure writing this book with you as my editor. Thank you for your support, your patience, and your great ideas for the direction of the content.

To Steve, my agent: Thank you for believing in *Sweet Potato Soul* and seeing the potential in my style of vegan soul food. It's been a long journey, and I'm so grateful for your patience and expertise along the way.

To my siblings and closest friends, for your unwavering support, for recipe tasting, and for keeping a smile on my face: DeMion Claiborne, Brandon Claiborne, Collin St. Dic, Lynzee Lawyer, Alisha Phillips, Julie Civiello, Eunice Woods, Isabelle Steichen, and Kristin Esposito.

To my recipe-testers, for your support, enthusiasm, time, and insights: JoDana Johnson-Newman, Federica Norreri, Christina Keeton, Cheryl van Grunsven, Krystle Watler, Loutrina Staley, Nzingah Oniwosan, Alexandra Charlemagne, Lisa Gonzales, Tangye Ward, Veronique Daoust, Will Nunnally, Deb Rowley, Quo Vardis Thompson, Emilie Hebert, Melinda Parkhurst, Michele Hoover, Cassia Charles, Kristin Z. Black.

To my yoga studio, Unity Yoga Harlem, and my teachers for supporting me spiritually, emotionally, and physically through this practice that I hold so dear. Thank you Sarah May, Chloe Mackenzie, Argentina Rosado, and Brenda Umana.

To my readers, viewers, and clients, without whom this book would not be possible: Thank you for your love and support, your feedback, and for trusting my recipes. You've helped me to become a better chef. You fill me with pride and joy.

To the worldwide vegan community for championing a cause built on compassion, kindness, humility, and generosity.

"All beings seek for happiness; so let your compassion extend itself to all." —Mahavamsa

INDEX

· · · · · · · · ·

ABOUT THE AUTHOR

JENNÉ CLAIBORNE is a vegan chef, cooking instructor, and the creator of *Sweet Potato Soul,* the blog and YouTube channel. She studied at the Institute for Integrative Nutrition and founded the personal chef company The Nourishing Vegan, whose clients have included India Arie, Lucy Liu, Lululemon, Soho House, Whole Foods, and many more. Her recipes and nutritional advice have been featured on NBC's *Today*, in *VegNews, Ebony,* Greatist.com, *Refinery 29,* BET, Well+Good, Shape.com, *Laika Magazine, Vegetarian Times, Thoughtfully Magazine,* InStyle.com, the *Huffington Post, Reader's Digest*, Urban Bush Babes, Main Street Vegan Radio, and *Our Hen House*. She is the cocreator of Buddhalicious, an eCourse that makes it easy for people to adopt a healthy and delicious vegan diet.